Somebody's Gonna Lose a Trailer

Gary Strakshus

Illustrated by Dr. Gary Simmons

PAGE PUBLISHING
Conneaut Lake, PA

First originally published by Page Publishing 2023

Illustrations by Gary Simmons

ISBN 979-8-88960-069-5 (pbk)
ISBN 979-8-88960-071-8 (digital)

Printed in the United States of America

CONTENTS

INTRODUCTION

I've been at this job for forty-plus years. Owning and managing trailer parks certainly wasn't what I thought I was going to do with my life. I'd graduated from college with a BS in recreation administration and had been voted into Kappa Delta Pi, an international honor society. Instead of running some park district, I found myself running a trailer park.

Doing this job can make an old man out of you. It is mostly a thankless, high-pressure, unappreciated, and extremely demanding job. Yet it can be remarkably rewarding. I look back now and realize that I have thoroughly enjoyed the experience. I am a better person for it.

The people and the situations I've run into have provided fodder for many a story through the years. Friends and family would say, "Hey, you should be writing that stuff down!" Year after year, more stories, more choruses of "Hey, you should be writing that stuff down!" No one would believe the things I've seen or had to handle.

There had been so many wild and crazy things that have happened through the years that I myself finally said, "Hey, I should be writing this stuff down!" So here it is. Welcome to my world in a book I'm calling *Somebody's Gonna Lose a Trailer*.

I blame my parents. My mom and dad, Al and Marjorie Strakshus, were married in 1948 and honeymooned in Hot Springs, Arkansas. They found the small Southern town friendly and quaint and the surrounding area beautiful, with its rolling green mountains and sparkling lakes. They vowed to one day to retire to Hot Springs and enjoy the remainder of their lives there.

In 1977, my father was one year from retiring from a job in Chicago that he had held for thirty years when he decided to start his search for a small income-producing property in Hot Springs, where he could do small projects and still enjoy retirement with a little extra money coming in. My dad sent my mom and me to locate the perfect investment. I had just graduated from college and wasn't really excited about any YMCA or park district job offers, so I happily accompanied my mom on this mission for their happy retirement future. We thought we'd look at small resorts or hotels in and around the Hot Springs area.

Nothing really filled the bill. Then we stumbled across a beautiful little trailer park, located right on Lake Hamilton, just a couple of miles out from Hot Springs. I knew this was *it*. My father made an offer, and because I had nothing lined up in the way of work, I agreed to run the place for him for a year or so until he retired. One year! How tough could that be?

My dad's signature on the closing papers wasn't dry before he found out that he had been downsized, and his big Chicago company had let him go. Fired! Miraculously, he was able to quickly secure a position with another company in Chicago, but he would have to work an additional ten years to be properly vested so he could retire with a pension. In that moment, one year became ten years for me, holding down the fort—or rather—park in Hot Springs. Keep in mind, I was a green college boy with no experience doing anything except homework and class projects. Managing a twenty-five-space mobile home park full of old people was not on any class curriculum description I had. On the other hand, I have always been drawn to challenging adventures, and moving 725 miles from home—alone— to manage a trailer park was right up my alley.

Collecting rent was a breeze. On the first of the month, the old folks were lined up at my door trying to be the first one to pay their rent. Every day a new problem would arise, and I would figure out a way to remedy the situation. Within a year, you could say I had earned my master's degree in plumbing, electrical, carpentry, roofing, siding, and interpersonal park relations by fixing all that needed fixing in the park. I also earned a "PhD" (usually known as "*P*iled *h*igher and *D*eeper," but in my case, *Posthole Digger*) because I actually wore out the old posthole digger as a result of all the fence and electric pole holes I dug.

Even though I was acclimating to my new job and new home, I missed my college sweetheart, Gay Groebe. We had been dating before I made the big move to Hot Springs. She was already working and building a stellar reputation as an advocate for young people. She had gotten her bachelor's degree in social work at our college. Because of her job and because all her family were in the Chicago area, I didn't feel as though I had the right to ask her to uproot her life to join me in Hot Springs. We had been staying in touch with phone calls, letters, and the occasional visit, but I wanted her with me full-time. There was only one thing to do: I popped the question, and she said "Yes!" So by the end of my first year in Hot Springs, I had my new wife with me. Life was made more perfect.

Within five years, this Yankee punk college boy was multilingual—able to understand and speak Southern, Spanglish, Hillbilly redneck, and black English. This feat was accomplished by interactions with the incredibly diverse population of Hot Springs.

Five years later, my dad finally retired, and my parents moved from Chicago to their retirement dream town. They moved into a vacant trailer at the park I later named the Python Trailer (more on that in the chapter on evictions).

Almost immediately, it was clear that my dad didn't really want to take over as manager of the trailer park. He had no interest in collecting rent. It took him days to fix something that would have taken me an hour, and he hated confrontation, avoiding most of the tenants like the plague. It was evident that he wanted true retirement: time to do what he wanted when he wanted to do it. So we agreed that I would stay on to manage the park, and my parents soon purchased a picture-perfect brick ranch right on the lake just five miles away.

I found that I loved every aspect of running a trailer park, and I thoroughly enjoyed living in Hot Springs. I particularly loved being my own boss, planning my own schedule and deciding what needed to be done each day, then setting about doing it in a quick and proper fashion. Or putting all the tasks aside and spending the morning catching my limit of fish with a longtime tenant, Monk (chapter 1).

I liked the lifestyle so much I made the decision to be a mobile home mogul for the rest of my life. Gay and I bought property south of town and developed another trailer park (oops! mobile home village, chapter 3). Soon after that, I bought my dad's trailer park from him. I've never regretted it. I loved the parks, the tenants, and the situations so much that I started to tell the stories that had happened in the first ten years of doing business. As I have said, people encouraged me to "write that stuff down!"

The events and people you will meet in this book are real, and I have recounted events as best as I can recollect. I have changed most of the names and have often substituted aliases that add flavor to the story. I've incorporated the different dialects I have encountered, and I've included a few off-color phrases that sometimes came from the people involved and sometimes came from me. I trust the reader will accept this as an attempt to describe the events in a more realistic and comedic manner.

One of my favorite parts of this whole process is sitting down with Gay once I have finished a story, having her proofread it, and reading it aloud to me. She is familiar with all the people and situations of my past, so she is able to read the stories with perfect effect and inflection. I love you, Gay.

My next favorite thing to do is watch as others read the stories. I have been known to bring my working manuscript on our vacations to Mexico. While lying around the pool, I would search out my next victim. My timing had to be just right: approaching someone who was just finishing a chapter in their book or their magazine article. First making small talk with this perfect stranger, I would then mention that I am writing a book and ask if they would be interested in reading what I had so far. Surprisingly, no one ever refused. I would hand over the copy, sit myself on the opposite side of the pool, and watch. Emotions would range from chuckles to tears to hard belly laughs. Some folks even made corrections and suggestions in the margins. I have also stayed in touch with some of those people over the years. Most of them are hungry for more unbelievable stories

from the quiet little trailer park in Hot Springs, Arkansas. As owner/
manager, I always oblige.

Now with this little book, I bring them to you.

CHAPTER 1

My Old People

Nothing good happens between 2:00 and 4:00 a.m.

The very worst thing to hear if you own a trailer park is "My trailer's on fire!" One night, between 2:00 and 4:00 a.m., eighty-year-old Lance Lipschitz, the upper half of my obnoxiously gay, geriatric tenants in space number 21 (Lance had decidedly more masculine energy than his partner, Chad) appeared at my front door, yelling,

"My trailer's on fire! My trailer's on fire!" I threw on some shorts and ran to number 21. Sure enough, Lance was right.

There I was—barefoot, half asleep in midwinter, staring at a mobile home burning. (It was my first, but I had heard that they go up very fast.) Thinking that Chad "Sweet Cheeks" Lovelady, the other half of the couple, was in the blazing home, I yelled into the door, "Chad, if you're in here, you better get your ass the hell out NOW!" Then I ran back to our house and attempted to call the fire department (this was before 911) and got ready to do battle with the fire. Donning pants, shirt, boots, and a jacket, I was ready to commence a firefight. This outfit became known as my emergency nighttime uniform.

Oh yeah, I must say that it's impossible to remember the phone number to the volunteer fire department in the early morning hours if you have *never* called it. This is true even if a list of emergency numbers is posted on the rotary phone from which you are calling. After a frantic search in the phone book, I finally got the volunteers on the way.

Running back to number 21 at a much faster pace with shoes afoot, I can tell you the inferno did not wait for me. It was now in every room and could be considered fully engulfed! The fire was so big that it was licking the homes on each side of it. My first thought was to pull down the curtains, which were burning. Bad idea! They fell and wrapped around my arm, causing much dismay and pain later.

My next brilliant plan was to kick the uprights that supported the awnings, causing them to fall in front of the trailer's doorways and the fire that was roaring out of them. This was actually an *excellent* idea because it stopped the fire from leaping to the homes on each side—and burning them to the ground—like it was well on its way to doing to unit number 21. It also gave the fire department time to arrive, join in the fun, set up, and do its thing on the blaze… but not before the home burned down to the frame.

What I learned from this experience was that one should (1) always have clothes close, at the ready, for any nighttime emergency; (2) never rent to goofball, electrically challenged guys who might wire the pilot ignite button on the heater to a permanent position (this was found to be the cause of the fire); and (3) when developing a mobile home park, be sure to space the homes far enough apart so if one burns, they all won't go up in flames.

There are several things of utmost importance to the elderly, two of which are mail delivery and bodily functions. There's no telling how many times I have hailed a "Good afternoon, Mr. So-and-So, how are you today?" Only to get a response like "Did the mail run yet?" Or even better, have the old fart tell me about the great BM he (or she) had that morning.

The one good thing about renting to the elderly is that you can count on getting the rent on the third of the month. This is when they get their Social Security checks, and each of them wants to be the first to get their rent paid in full. Not that I'm complaining, but young people should take a lesson in paying the rent on time.

Another unusual phenomenon of the elderly is if they see you doing a chore like washing your car, raking your yard, or trimming your hedge, they want their car washed, their yard raked, or their hedge trimmed. But the greater observation is that when I end up doing the chore for them, they want to reimburse my kindness with not money but food offerings. I have received many pies, cakes, cookies, and even meat loafs (for larger jobs) in compensation for my time and labor. Some of the old-timers are actually very good cooks. As for the others—whose culinary talents are not quite up to snuff—I'd just like to say, "Show me the money."

A drawback of renting to octogenarians is, well, they die. One by one, gone. After a couple of years, this occurred so often that my wife and I started to bet each other over which tenant would be the next to kick the bucket. We actually got very good at predicting which one was next to meet his Maker. In the first twenty years that we have owned the park, we figured that we've lost over thirty tenants to the grim reaper.

One of the more memorable deaths was that of a very nice, one-armed fisherman by the name of Al Hook in unit number 19. Mr. Hook would occasionally take me out fishing with him, and we always had good luck. This guy also loved to bet the ponies at the local track. In addition, Al liked to have an adult beverage…or two…or three…while wagering.

On one particular day, he made it home only to pass out on the floor of his bedroom, aspirate his vomit, and die. His wife, Alberta, found him this way and came running to me for help. Having been trained in advanced first aid and emergency care, I, of course, immediately knew that Al was gone. He had no pulse. His face was blue in color, and he was getting a bit stiff. Mrs. Hook, the loving wife, was yelling at me to "do something, *anything*!"

Knowing he was on the other side but not wanting to disappoint the frantic lady, I commenced to give the corpse CPR. With each breath into his mouth, I could hear gurgling from Mr. H's chest. I tried so hard to massage his heart that I heard and felt ribs break. When the EMTs got there, they told me that I had done all that I could. This was one death that no one expected and probably hit me the hardest. He was a good old guy, and I hope that he is looking down on us while sitting in his twelve-foot aluminum fishing boat and holding winning tickets in his one good hand.

Another memorable, alcohol-related death occurred in rental number 22. This was another nice old man, Ted Gentleheimer, who had lost his wife from natural causes several years earlier.

Separately, but in the same time frame, we had rented our smallest home to a tenant named Alice "The Black Widow" Cates, a petite little lady (who turned out to be as crazy as bat shit!).

The stage was set!

Alice discovered that old man Ted was lonely after the loss of his wife, and she jumped at the opportunity to befriend him. Alice must have thought that Ted had some money because she just about moved in with him, spending all their time together in his home. What they spent most of their time doing was drinking. This went on all day and all night for several weeks. She stopped paying the rent on her unit, but all her belongings were still in it.

When I began to put heavy pressure on her to pay the rent, Alice put her master plan into effect. That plan, as I saw it, was to get Mr. G so drunk that he would agree to let her move in, and they would then share his wealth. It didn't actually work out the way she had hoped.

Between 2:00 and 4:00 a.m., Alice came pounding on my door, saying that she thought something was wrong with her drinking buddy, Mr. Gentleheimer. After donning my emergency nighttime uniform, I ran to investigate the condition of Mr. G. The house reeked of alcohol, and there was the old man, lying on his bed, deader than Julius Caesar. When the EMTs got there, they said that he had been dead for many hours. Rigor mortis had set in, and he was as stiff as a board. In fact, he was so rigid that when we carried him out of the trailer, we had to snap him into a jackknife position to the right to get him into the hall from the bedroom. Then we had to snap him to the left to get him out the back door to the waiting meat wagon.

The cause of death was found to be alcohol poisoning. Alice had poured enough booze down Mr. G to kill him and then just left. I kicked the pathetic, murdering bitch out the next day!

One death…which I will never forget…was that of Austin Seacrest. My memory of him stands out not for his death but for his *post*death goings-on. Muriel, his wife, and Austin lived in space number 6, right on the lake. Their time was spent sitting in their loungers, watching the TV, and smoking cigarettes. The couple had a great view of the lake during commercials. Austin's health was not good, and they had been discussing his inevitable demise. Both agreed when he died, his ashes would be dumped in the lake within the view afforded by their living room window. This agreement was made without my knowledge.

Months later, he did indeed pass. Two weeks after his demise, I was cutting the grass when the mailman approached me and said he had a package from a funeral home for Austin Seacrest. I looked at the postman, smiled, pointed at the parcel, and said, "No, that *is* Austin Seacrest."

The next day, I was recruited by Mrs. S to hold a burial at sea. Now this kind of thing was new to me. I had never seen or held a cremated body in my hands. After putting Austin (in the plastic box) in my boat, it was off to the center of the lake. With directions from Mrs. S from the shore, I stopped the boat and threw the box into the water. It floated! Retrieving the box with a paddle, I then opened the box and found a plastic bag. I tossed it into the lake. It floated! Retrieving the bag, I examined it. The box was filled with brown, chunky pieces of Austin (not the ashes or dust that I was expecting). The only thing left to do was to tear open the bag and dump it. All this occurred on the other side of the boat from Mrs. S's vision, so she never knew the circus-like burial I was giving her husband. All in all, for my first aquatic funeral, it went quite well.

Several years later, I received *Mrs.* Seacrest by mail. Just before her demise, she had discussed plans for her final resting place with me. Now being somewhat of an expert in maritime funerals, I agreed to reunite the two for all eternity. Gathering some friends and family for a day of fun on the lake, I rented a party barge, and the stage was set. (I'm not sure if I mentioned anything to them about the cremated body in the plastic box.) Anyway, when we got to the general location of Mr. S's resting place, I killed the engine, announced my intentions, said a few holy words, and dumped the chunks over the side. It was a beautiful and touching ceremony.

RIP, Mr. and Mrs. S.

When dealing with a geriatric bunch of people, dementia (this was before Alzheimer's) is bound to pop up now and again. Evidence of this occurred one day when Ray "BM" Favorite, from number 2, informed me that he did his hitch in the service (WWI) with Henry Mancini. When he suspected that I did not truly believe him, Ray said that he had absolute proof to back his statement. After rummaging around in a closet for about thirty minutes, he came out with an old picture. Sure enough, it was of two guys, in WWI garb, standing next to each other. Ray pointed to one guy and said, "That's me, and the other guy is Henry Mancini."

Not that I didn't believe Mr. Favorite, but the problem I had was that the picture was of two men wearing full gas masks. The best thing to do in situations like this is to just let it go.

Who knows, maybe it really was Henry Mancini!

Harry "Happy Man" Able, of number 13, was an avid fisherman. Another nice old man with a boat of his own, and he used it regularly. During the many years that Harry stayed with us, I don't recall him ever bringing a fish back to the dock. Harry would walk past our house each day, just about the same time. He would leave the boat dock and head to the same choice spot every day and then head back home one hour later. This guy was like clockwork, five days a week. He would fish for one solid hour, catch nothing, and then head home. This might be diagnosed as dementia or just a severe case of optimism—who's to say? Now my wife, who is a psychotherapist, says, "To do the same thing over and over again and expect different results is the definition of insanity." My take on this behavior is that Harry, although a bit goofy, was one of happiest, sweetest guys I ever met. He didn't need to catch a fish; he was fishing, and that was all that mattered to him. The fact he made it back to the dock each day was a miracle in itself.

Another resident of the park who had visions of being a great angler was Harold "Knothead" Hilliard, from space number 21. Harold lived with us until his demise, way before we rented to the wacko homosexuals who burned the place down. Not being a doctor or psychologist myself, I still feel safe to say that Mr. H wallowed in a state of dementia and was perpetually confused. Each day, Harold would walk down to the fishing dock, fish for ten minutes, and then walk back up the hill to his house. Often I would ask him how he did. He had many answers to my query, like "They ain't bitin' today…," "Dropped my pole in the lake…," "Forgot my pole…," or "Forgot my bait."

One day, I noticed a lump on his forehead and asked Harold about it. He said that he had not noticed it. Each day thereafter, I noticed the lump getting bigger and bigger. His state of confusion grew equally with the lump.

Not long after I noticed the lump, Harold showed up with a boat from somewhere and was determined to venture onto the lake to fish. I convinced him to let me go with him. Nothing is worse than losing a paying tenant to a mysterious boating incident. Off we went, with Harold all excited to see new fishing grounds. Ten minutes out, his time limit, he pulled over to the bank to wet a line. Ten minutes later, he was ready to head back.

Just before we started our return trip, Harold told me he had put a new propeller on the motor that morning. In my mind, I'm thinking, *This can't be good,* but I figured we had made it this far, so we were probably okay. But as soon as he put the motor in reverse, nothing happened. Then it hit me what had gone awry. In changing the prop, Harold had neglected to reinstall the cotter pin back correctly into the prop. As long as we were going forward, it would stay put, pushing itself toward the shaft. When shifting into reverse, there was nothing to keep the propeller from spinning off the shaft and into the deep, dark depths of the lake. I made my way to the back of the boat and raised the motor out of the water. Sure enough, no prop. So there we were—stranded—with no prop, no paddles, no oars, and no options other than waving and screaming at any boaters that may pass our way.

Just about dark, a good Samaritan noticed our dilemma and headed our direction. He towed us back to our dock, where Harold vowed to "never mess with the lake again." A short time after this incident, Harold H. died from a brain tumor.

The lesson learned was to see your doctor on a regular basis, especially if you have a large growth on your face.

The person most responsible for elevating my extensive fishing skills to their current level (and they're at a very high level—just ask me!) would be my tenant in number 10, Mr. Monk Boatman. He was one of the best live-bait anglers on Lake Hamilton. Monk caught more fish than any other five people combined.

In his nineties, Monk took me under his wing (fin?) and taught me the ropes of live-bait fishing. About once a week, we would go out to a nearby creek, turn over some rocks, and catch live crawdads. In one hour, between the two of us, we could snag about three hundred of these crawling crustaceans (the bass just love 'em). Arriving back at the trailer park, we would stow most of the mudbugs in a live-bait tank, taking a few dozen with us to the boat. (Monk's boat was a real antique, a decrepit, twelve-foot wooden V-bottom.)

Off we would go to one of Monk's rocky-point honey holes in the lake. Hooking the crawdad through the tail, he taught me how to cast away from the bank and slowly retrieve the bait. When you feel a bite, set the hook by quickly raising the rod tip straight up. "Don't drop your tip, don't drop your tip," I can still hear these words…as he said them to me hundreds of times. When I would miss a fish, Monk would of course say, "You dropped your tip." He was always right. When I didn't drop my tip and we caught our limit of fish, we would head back to the dock to clean them.

Now Monk always claimed to be an American Indian. But I always found it strange that he cleaned fish with an electric knife. I always thought he was Irish, but who is to say? He taught me how to filet a fish with an electric knife, guaranteed no bones. This was a good thing, because my wife wouldn't let me bring a fish with bones into the house. Anyway, catch 'em, clean 'em, cook 'em, and eat 'em!

Thanks, Monk, I hope you're proud of me for catching many four- and five-pound small-mouthed bass on my recent trip to Canada. I know that you are one of the best fishermen in the happy hunting grounds (or friendly fishing grounds?), and remember, "DON'T DROP YOUR TIP!"

When operating a trailer park, as manager, you will inevitably run into situations that involve drugs, alcohol, guns, and what I like to call D students. Although none of my D students were involved in the perpetrating of this next event, one of them was indeed the victim.

At 2:30 a.m., Alberta Hook in number 19 (the widow of Al, the one-armed fisherman who died in his vomit), woke us from a deep slumber. She said that she thought she'd heard what sounded like a gunshot and wanted me to investigate. Taking a stroll around the park, I noticed nothing out of the ordinary. Asking if she was okay, Alberta assured us she was. When inquiring about the abrasion on her cheek, Alberta said she probably scratched herself with a finger-nail. So we all went back to bed.

The next day, I decided to check on Alberta. She said she was fine, but there was a hole in her headboard that hadn't been there yesterday. Upon inspection of the headboard, there was indeed a hole the size of a dime. Pulling the bed away from the wall, we discovered another hole all the way through the trailer. Looking out the window of the trailer, we saw a hole in the window of the apartment on the property next door. Being an expert in forensic science, I lined up the hole in the window of the apartment…to the hole through the trailer wall…to the hole in the headboard. We did what CSI would do. We envisioned a straight line across the room to the wall at the foot of the bed. Bingo, another hole! On the other side of this wall was the heater. Sure enough, embedded in the heater was a large-caliber projectile (a bullet).

While waiting for the sheriff's department to arrive and investigate, we came to the conclusion that if Mrs. Hook had had a pillow under her head during the night, she would be dead. That's when Alberta absolutely lost it! The scratch on her cheek was where the bullet had grazed her. It was found that drugs, alcohol, a gun, and a lot of stupidity were all involved. The jerk was arrested, and Alberta, after being convinced that a near miss was as good as a miss by a mile, finally calmed down.

CHAPTER 2

Pests

So far, these stories have been about the people who were inherited when we bought the park. What happens when old tenants die is they leave a void, which in the rental business, has to be filled. Finding more ancient folks to fill this void would be a good choice, but it's not always easy to do. The ads placed in the local paper are not usually answered by the mature generation. So you end up renting to a much younger crowd, a choice, although necessary in many cases, we would often live to regret.

With a rash of tenants going to meet their Maker in a several-months span, we decided to bite the bullet and try a new approach. Michael S. answered our ad for trailer rentals. At the time, we had several available and were quite anxious to get them filled. Michael came with his parents (a red flag, we decided later), and we chose to rent him number 7, our nicest home on the lake. His parents told us what a nice, clean, and quiet boy their son was. It was our assumption they were talking about Michael, the son they brought with them. Anyway, the home they chose was right next to ours, so we reckoned that we could keep an eye on young Michael. We did the deal, signed the lease, and got rent and deposit from the parents. This should have been another red flag!

Immediately after the parents left, we started seeing carloads of young kids coming and going from space number 7. Our thought was they were helping their friend Mike move in his stuff. Weeks later, the traffic got progressively worse. Day and night, young folks were coming and going. Complaints from other tenants began flowing to us, "Them younguns are disturbing the peace." And I had to agree. Warnings from me went through one ear and out the other. If anything, it got even worse.

One particular day, I had had enough. Cars were backed up five to six deep. The noise level was that of a full-blown bachelor party. This was in the middle of the day, and I figured if there was a party going on, I was going to invite myself. Walking next door, I peered through the glass door and discovered a house full of teenage boys, large quantities of beer, and porn on the big screen.

Sending the little boys on their way, Michael and I had a heart-to-heart talk. He assured me that things would be different in the future and there would be no more parties. When I asked him about the numerous terrariums scattered around, he said they were for his scorpions, tarantulas, and mice. I reminded him of the no-pet rule, but he begged to keep them as long as these creepy crawlers would stay in their glass homes. The agreement came against my better judgment. *Always* rely on your better judgment!

The following weeks showed no letup in the traffic and out-of-control young people. The only solution was to hand Mike my first ever eviction notice (the first of many) called a notice to quit. Not knowing about a *ten*-day notice to quit, which is legal in our state, I gave Michael a *thirty*-day notice to quit. My bad, ignorant me! Twenty-nine days passed before we saw any sign of movement on his part. On the thirtieth day, Michael and friends loaded packed boxes into cars all day and into the night.

The weather at that time was some of the worst on record with thunderstorms, high winds, and horrible lightning strikes. It must have been around midnight when I decided to go next door to see if Michael had indeed vacated. On his last trip out, Mike apparently had flipped the electric breaker, because there were no lights. Feeling my way from room to room, I could only see whenever there was a lightning strike. I noticed that there were only a few items left in the house.

Opening the door to the master bedroom, I sensed something at my feet. The next bolt of lightning permitted me to get a peek at what it was. The snake's head was inches from my feet, with the rest of the body stretching the length of the room. The tail was somewhere in the master bathroom. Now this home is a fourteen-by-seventy-footer, and the bedroom is at least twelve feet deep. You do the math. The serpent was at least twelve feet long or more. Slamming the door, I nearly killed myself running back through the trailer to get outside and back to my house.

When Michael came back the next day to pick up his last load, I told him I had inspected his home the previous night. My question to him was, "Did I really see what I thought I saw?"

He confirmed it was indeed a thirteen-foot python named Snuggles.

I asked out of pure curiosity, "Is it dangerous?"

He replied, "Only when it's hungry and it hasn't eaten in quite some time."

Then Michael left, off to his next unsuspecting landlord. When the cleaning crew (my wife and I) cleaned the home in anticipation of the next renter, we found…under the bed…the discarded skin of the thirteen-foot slithering monster, which still haunts me to this day.

I began to miss my old people.

Pest control is a pretty big deal in a trailer park. If you are not attentive, you can be overrun with a variety of unwanted pests. Living in the South, we are all acquainted with what is known as the water bug. This creepy nuisance is actually an American roach. (Please don't inform any of my tenants of this fact. As long as it is known as a water bug, people don't freak out so much.)

Occasionally, a unit will become overrun with these nasty creatures. When this happens, all we do is place a call to the bug man, Dr. Bell. We have been using him for over thirty years and always look forward to his visits. Jim makes a point of hitting all my rentals every three months. This also gives me the opportunity to see the condition of each unit on a quarterly basis. On these visits, we usually change out the heat and air filters and check for any repairs that might be needed. On many occasions the bug man has witnessed me cuss out and tongue-lash a tenant for trashing my place. Countless times, Jim has actually sprayed around people still in their bed at 11:00 a.m. Dr. Bell shows no mercy for D students with no job and no ambition. All the while he is spraying, he is telling me the joke of the day.

I love this guy.

On occasion, a pest other than a water bug will find its way into a home. My tenant in number 8, Buddy B., told me that he was hearing noises in his unit during the night. After numerous times trying to close up all the obvious entry points and not knowing what we were dealing with, if anything, I just about gave up.

One morning, Buddy came to me and stated that he had eradicated the offender in his home. Asking him what flavor varmint it was, he said it was an opossum. Of course my next question was, "Did you shoot it? How did you kill it?"

All Buddy said was, "Seven iron."

It turned out that Mr. B. was an avid golfer, and his weapon of choice happened to be close at hand, as he had a 7:00 a.m. tee time that morning.

Bugs, snakes, and very young men are not alone in the category of trailer park nuisances. For some reason, trailer parks are like a magnet for stray cats. It is a fact that unwanted pets are disposed of by dropping them off in our park. I suppose the thought is that the ex-pet will be taken care of by the inhabitants of a beautiful, safe, and quiet community such as ours. Little do they know of the no-pet policy in my lease agreement. I actually train my tenants not to befriend, feed, or let the strays in their homes.

Problems that inevitably occur include garbage cans dumped and trash strewn everywhere, vinyl car roofs used as cat scratchers, and the worst thing, procreation of felines. The toms will do what they know to do and mate with the lady cats. The females will find a nice, warm, and dry place under trailers and make their nest up in the insulation of the homes. This not only creates a mess but also introduces fleas and ticks to my rentals.

One year there was an unusual number of drop-offs. The task of animal control was added to my job description. Catching my first unwanted cat in a live trap, I relocated the pest five miles down the road from our park. Congratulating myself for coming up with what I thought was the perfect solution to our problem was short-lived. Two days later, the damn thing showed back up in the park.

Repeating the process of capturing it in the live trap (tuna fish was the preferred bait for this kitty), I then got the brilliant idea of delivering the furry troublemaker down the road to a friend's house. I left it on the front porch with a good helping of tuna fish and wished it good luck. Years later, I found out that the cat had stuck around and became the favorite family pet. It turned out that their young child had been asking for a cute little kitty, and this one fit the bill. I never told them the truth.

Creative evictions have gotten to be one of my specialties. After years of letting the tenants run over me and pretty much get their way, I decided enough was enough. So I came up with ways to rid myself of pests of the human variety. One technique consisted of using a pest to get rid of a pest.

Tenants in number 18, Emily R. and her girlfriend (a Lebanese couple) were breaking rules and not paying the rent. After I had posted a ten-day notice to quit on their door, they informed me that it would take longer than that to get all their stuff out and find new accommodations. About that time, they told me that there was a horrible smell coming into their house from under the trailer. Upon investigation, I discovered that a skunk had made her home in the insulation under number 18.

The people at Critter Getters, a local pest-removal business, were very helpful, saying they could come right out and apprehend the offender. They said that the female skunk would continue to spray each night, attracting the male portion of the pair. Thanking them for their information, I told them to wait to hear from me.

Thus was borne a new form of creative eviction. I explained to the unhappy couple in number 18 that I couldn't afford to eradicate the skunk problem because they didn't pay the rent. They were gone the next day. Critter Getters trapped the lady skunk the day after that.

My only wish is that I had a pet skunk that would spray on demand.

DANGEROUS pests have popped up every now and then in the trailer park. Fortunately, though, they have been few and far between. The list of dangerous intruders includes vicious stray dogs, rabid bats, skunks, and West Nile virus-infected mosquitoes. All the aforementioned have the possibility of causing illness or worse... *death*. All these creatures have made an appearance in our park and have been dealt with.

One particularly very dangerous, uninvited guest was discovered during a remodel of an old farmhouse, which was on the property and which we had recently purchased. Whenever tenants move out, we usually take a close look at the unit and decide what we can do to make it more attractive. The home became vacant, and the decision was to do a complete overhaul. This included adding a new roof, extending the front bedroom and kitchen, moving the laundry room and water heater, laying vinyl on floors, and, of course, putting fresh paint on all the walls.

In moving the laundry room and water heater, it was necessary to switch the plumbing around under the house. The house was originally built around the turn of the century, and the crawl space was very tight. A large plumber could not go where I was headed. So I found an access along the foundation and began to inch my way to begin plumbing relocation. With flashlight in my mouth and making my way inch by inch in the darkness, I felt something crawling from under me…to in front of me. Pointing the light one foot ahead, I saw—to my horror—a *copperhead* snake! Backing out like I was shot from a rocket, I vowed never to return.

I thought it best if I could find a skinny plumber listed in the yellow pages.

CHAPTER 3

TLIs and Evictions

TLI is an abbreviation for "Tenant left it!" This term came about years ago when I was asked about a piece of clothing I was wearing, and I replied, "Tenant left it." As a matter of fact, most of the work clothes and a great deal of the dress clothes I wear come from the piles of stuff left by tenants. I get first shot at the good stuff abandoned by people, so I figure if it fits or I can use a piece of furniture or whatever, why not? After all, I am a firm believer in recycling.

It's often funny how the amount of back rent a tenant owes me correlates directly to the amount of crapola they leave. It's amazing what people leave. Sometimes the value of the stuff left outweighs the balance due. When this happens, I can only assume that they're thinking they are paid in full. I, on the other hand, don't see it that way. After picking through the mountains of treasures, keeping what I think I can use, I then have to haul the rest of the junk to either charities, stores, or the dump.

Furnishings that could be considered TLI include couches, loungers, kitchen sets, end tables, lamps, beds, nightstands, washers, dryers, linens, towels (one of my favorite items), microwaves, televisions, radios, computers, and refrigerators. In years past, several units were left with some assortment of all these things. Considering they would have to replace all these items, it makes one wonder if these folks were just looking for a new start. Or better yet, they probably found a new landlord to mooch off and one who was willing to furnish them with what they needed. In the end, this won't work because I've found that renters are more likely to take better care of their own things, not giving a hoot about the condition of items furnished to them.

I have already touched on the subject of clothes being left. It's a little known fact when looking at a prospective tenant, I consider their size. Why not? If they wear a medium shirt, size 31-by-31 jeans, and an 8 1/2 shoe, the chances of them leaving clothes that will fit me when they split are good. All my work jackets are TLI, including hoodies, windbreakers, and rain gear. Even hats, gloves, socks, and occasionally underwear find their way into my dresser drawers. Personal items included in the TLI collection are prescription eyeglasses, towels (did I mention that this is my favorite TLI item?), toothbrushes, all forms of toiletries, wheelchairs, walkers, porta-potties, and a prosthetic leg. (I believe it was a right-leg amputation at the knee.)

Many of the tools in my arsenal to repair and maintain my fleet of rentals are TLIs. Literally hundreds of screwdrivers, hammers, saws, levels, drills, bits, wrenches, jacks, paintbrushes, rollers, paint trays, and tarps have been found abandoned. Even chain saws have been left, enabling me to take care of the tree trimming in the park.

Ex-tenants can be very generous, since porno and sex toys are a very popular form of TLI. It seems people forget their hiding places for dirty magazines. I have found them under mattresses, on top of closet shelves, and under drawers. All forms of DVDs, such as guy on girl, girl on girl, two girls on guy, two girls on two guys, and two guys on one girl have been found discarded in empty rentals. There are even some homosexual variety videos like guy on guy (not my favorite), girl on girl (one of my favorites), and, of course, guy on guy on guy (yuck!). TLI sex toys and aides include vibrators, blow-up dolls, masks, chains, boots, lubricants, crotchless panties, scented candles, and dildos. One time, when I told my wife I found a dildo in a unit, she said, "I hope you didn't touch it. You don't know where it has been."

I, of course, replied, "Oh yes, I do!"

The record for the largest amount of stuff left behind goes to Sarah "Free-Bush" Goodbody and her boyfriend, Danny, in unit number 8.

First, a little background on these two idiots. I remember how the two of them were both drunk on their initial interview. This should have been a giant red flag for me, but… I let it pass. (I found out later that they were coming directly from another trailer park across town from which they were being evicted.) Cautiously accepting their application, I welcomed them into our little community. Big mistake! (It pays to do background checks.) The second red flag went off when they pulled up to their new home with a U-Haul, which was slam full of crap and bigger than the place they were renting. Again, they were so drunk that they had to enlist one of my tenants to help back the truck and empty its contents.

After the truck had been unloaded, there was only a narrow path from the front door to the back bedroom——an instant hoarder's haven. This is the way it stayed until I had them evicted. But I get ahead of myself.

Initially, Sarah and Danny had their minor run-ins with me. Loud fights, bothering others for cigarettes, alcohol, and rides to the liquor store were the reasons for complaints about them. It seems they came without a vehicle. (They should have kept the U-Haul.)

The first time I had Sarah arrested was when I got a call at 2:00 a.m. with a complaint of a drunk woman breaking the windows of the family in number 12. It seems Sarah was trying to break into the house, where she thought she had been partying earlier. The family had two small children and had been asleep for hours.

So I donned my emergency nighttime uniform and began my search for the offender, who I highly suspected was the new arrival in number 8. As I drove around the park, I saw Sarah run around the corner of unit *number 14*, which was below number 12, and occupied by a Vietnamese family. In hot pursuit, I chased her through the front door of number 14. She went right into the living room and down the hall, making a turn at the laundry room and trying to escape using the back door. After fumbling with the lock and not knowing what was on the other side of the door (I wasn't going to tell her), she stepped out to a ten-foot drop. Executing a perfect super-woman maneuver and landing on her face, Sarah lay there moaning. I jumped down and stood above her, straddling her head with my feet firmly on her long blonde hair. Dialing 911 on my cell phone, I held this position until the sheriff's deputy arrived. She then went off to jail. The fact that the deputy was very familiar with Sarah was not comforting to me. After filing charges and appearing in court, the judge granted damages to me and gave Ms. Sarah a no-trespass order.

I thought I had seen the last of her—*not!* The next time I had her arrested was when my own sister, who is two years younger than me and had recently moved into space number 30, called at 2:00 a.m., saying there was a naked woman on her front porch who was trying to get into her house. This was only one week after the last incident, so again jumping into my same emergency nighttime clothes, I ran down the hill to number 30.

Sure enough, there was Sarah, naked as the day she was born, lying flat plastered on the porch. It was then I realized that the only thing unattractive about Sarah was her utter drunkenness. Using this to my advantage when dialing 911, I happened to mention we had a disturbance involving a good-looking, totally naked, intoxicated woman. In record time, the sheriff's department sent three units to handle the situation. It seemed the six deputies were a bit disappointed I had wrapped Ms. Sarah in a beach towel before they got to the scene of the crime. Oh well, off to jail she went. Again!

The next time I had Sarah arrested was about a week later. Ignoring the no-trespass order by the judge, I witnessed her on the property. She apparently had had a long day of partying on the lake and was in her perpetual drunk condition, wearing only a skimpy bikini. Seeing me and not wanting to talk about the situation, Sarah ran off the property and onto the highway.

So I went back to my newly developed, supereffective MO and reported a good-looking, drunken female in a bikini, walking down the middle of the highway and blocking traffic. Once again, this got the sheriff deputies there on the double. When I appeared in court concerning the new charges, the judge recognized me as "the guy with the naked woman in the trailer park."

I, of course, corrected the judge, stating, "Mobile home village, Your Honor." It just had a better ring to it.

The fourth and final time I had the lovely Sarah arrested was a week later when I saw her in the park yet again. Boyfriend Danny was in the process of moving after my stern suggestion and a ten-day notice to quit. Sarah, I suppose, was there against court orders to help with the eviction.

For old time's sake, I thought I would introduce Lady Sarah to law enforcement one last time. When the deputies arrived, she had disappeared. Asked by the deputies where she was, Danny said she wasn't there. I told them if *he* was there, *she* was there and gave them permission to search the home. With all the junk in the house, there weren't many places to hide. Slowly down the trail to the bedroom, the deputies made their way and found her under the bed. She was of course…inebriated…but this time fully clothed.

At our final court appearance, the judge sentenced Sarah to a one-year term in a drug and alcohol dependency facility. He also said that I now owned all the stuff in the house, which Danny and Sarah had abandoned. This was all right with me because Danny was the same size as me and Sarah was the same size as my wife. A lifetime of

TLI work clothes, some of my dress clothes, and several emergency nighttime uniforms were donated by the couple who stayed with us for only two months. My wife really looks good in her TLI bikini.

A short time after her release from rehab, Sarah must have landed a job because I was sent a reimbursement check for all the damage she had caused and even for the towel I had wrapped her in.

Good luck, Sarah, I hope you get your life in order.

When Harley Dipschitz and his motorcycle momma, Mandy, parked in front of my office, my antenna should have gone up. They were riding a very loud, beat-up, filthy bike, wearing dirty clothes, and looking horribly unkempt. I was hoping they'd only ask for directions. No such luck. What the two Dipschitzes needed was a place to live.

Being very anxious to rent one of the several units we had available and being an equal-opportunity landlord, I again ignored all the alarms going off in my head and reluctantly let them sign a six-month lease. They fell in love with the aforementioned three-bedroom, two-bath farmhouse (with the snake still presumably under it), which we had just remodeled.

Soon after their arrival, I began to notice (or rather hear) the distinct, loud thundering of many Harley-Davidson motorcycles. The day I witnessed a half-dozen motorcycle mommas walking about and lying in the yard, clad only in thongs, I decided to make my first suggestion. I explained to them that this was a family park, and if their girlfriends wanted to run around dressed like they were—or rather *un*dressed like they were—maybe they should go to the beach.

The Dipschitzes met my concerns with deaf ears. Traffic picked up all day and night, and it seemed like none of their friends drove an actual car. More complaints were made by me, with the same results. When I began to get concerns from other residents of the park, I decided I was not going to lose good tenants because of bad ones.

Walking up to the biker gang house, I was greeted by two very large, drunk, leather-clad dudes. Something about them led me to believe they were acting as doormen or possibly bouncers. My high-alert sensor is usually spot-on, and it was currently at Mach-10 with these guys. This was semiconfirmed when I told them I was the land-lord, wanting to see Harley and Mandy.

One of them put his big paw on my shoulder and squeezed. Having been trained in the martial arts, my reflexes got the better of me. Feeling threatened and being assaulted by the paw, my backhand shot out, hitting the biker-bouncer square on the nose with good force. He ran into the house with a bloody proboscis, and his twin disappeared to tell Harley and Mandy what I had just done. They soon came to the door, where I handed them a ten-day notice to quit. None of them called the cops for the assault I committed, I can only assume, because of all the wants and warrants already sitting in the house. *I* didn't call because, after all, *I* am the cop of the park.

A few days later, loud music was emanating from the farm-house, disturbing the peace. There were no bouncers at the door, so I knocked. Hearing a loud, "Come in," I did. Walking into a room filled with card-playing, cigar-smoking, beer-drinking badasses, I felt a bit outnumbered. When one of them boldly asked, "What the hell do you want?"

I grabbed a steak knife from the counter and let it fly in his direction. The cutlery stuck in the wall next to the guy's head, about eyeball high. (I don't believe I have mentioned I have perfected the art of knife, dart, and shuriken throwing.) Anyway, an eerie quiet filled the room. So I said, "I WANT YOU ALL TO LEAVE NOW!"

Two days later, the final night on their ten-day notice, I went over to see how the progress of the move was coming along. Nearing the home, I smelled a peculiar chemical odor. Right away, I suspected a meth lab. After all, we *are* a trailer park in Arkansas… What else could it be? This put me on high alert, because like the joke goes:

Question: "What do a meth lab and an Arkansas
divorce have in common?"
Answer: *"Somebody's gonna lose a trailer."*

I must have startled the chemist in the kitchen when he saw me looking through the window. Something was dropped, kicked, or spilled, followed by an explosion and a blinding flash. When my vision came back, I saw what was left of the biker gang, jumping on their rides—some of them still smoldering—tearing into the night, never to be seen again.

A few cans of paint, some new vinyl, and the home was ready for my next better-chosen tenants. Although this was a tough, scary, and potentially dangerous eviction, I will admit, I do miss the mommas in their thongs. It kind of reminded me of the good old days in the seventies—sex, drugs, and rock and roll!

CHAPTER 4

More Evictions

Although often uncomfortable, evictions are an important and legal part of being a landlord. Serving of an eviction notice can be avoided by making good choices upon first contact with the prospective renter. First impressions can be a determining factor, and a landlord should go with his gut feeling. A person's appearance, their cleanliness, their manner of dress, the vehicle they drive, and the condition of it (inside and out) should all be considered when making the decision of whether or not you want to take them on as residents. Several times, I have actually followed the applicants back to their current residence just to check on their living conditions. If you drive to a bad neighborhood, see them pull into a yard strewn with trash, kids' toys, and dogs, you should turn around, go home, and lose their application.

Another unforgettable eviction was that of Rodney "No Luck" Potlicker, his wife Laura, and two teenage children. Number 35 was a perfect fit for them. It was a three-bedroom, two-bath, which I had recently picked up through a repo agency. The previous owner couldn't afford the mortgage, so she let it go back to the bank and moved home to Wisconsin. When I bought the place, I thought $7,500 for a three and two was an excellent price. Little did I know the work that was going to be necessary to get the place into shape in order to rent.

But before we get to Rodney and co, a little background on the previous owner, Debbie Mussyhausen, is needed. Debbie was a cat lady and a hoarder. She had lived in the park for three years. Upon inspection of the home after she had relocated, I discovered rooms full of trash. She never had used the trash service, which is provided by the county and paid for by me. In addition, Ms. Debbie had housed at least a dozen cats but never cleaned the litter boxes. I guess the cats got tired of the knee-high junk piled in their litter boxes and just did their business anytime and anywhere the need to go hit them. Needless to say, the smell was overpowering.

Armed with rakes, shovels, respirator masks, and hundreds of garbage bags, we began to literally dig our way through the home. It was very disturbing and disheartening to find the bodies of many kitty carcasses. The deeper we dug, the more we found. We had no idea Debbie was living this way because we were never invited into her home. I should have gotten a clue when I looked into her car window and saw cigarette butts at least six inches deep. It made me feel so bad we were so blind to the living conditions of this poor lady. After all, my wife is a social worker and therapist with many resources. We could have helped with her problem but really didn't know the extent of her situation. We always thought Debbie was just a little quirky. (Note to self: in the future, pay closer attention to the needs and actions of those around you.)

Now we can go back to Rodney. After a month of renovation, the unit was again habitable. When Rodney, Laura, and family moved in, we soon discovered that Rodney was pretty much a screwup. He held many jobs for a short time but then was dismissed or fired. The first job he lost was driving a trash hauler for the county (would've come in handy when Debbie lived here). The pickup of trash is very time oriented, and people like to have their garbage picked up at a certain time each week. Rodney could not meet the needs of the county's customers or his employer. A faulty alarm clock, a habit of running his truck off the road, and car trouble were all excuses Rodney used on the path to getting canned.

Collecting unemployment for months, Rodney finally found his next calling as a chef in a nearby restaurant. It seemed to be working for him until the restaurant's owner, Jason, a well-muscled, tattooed, shirtless ex-con, appeared at our door, wanting to know where "Chef Rodney" lived. He explained, not only was Rodney stealing food from the kitchen of the restaurant, but he was also taking money from the cash register. Jason, a fellow business owner and acquaintance of mine, was here to do bodily harm to Rodney. Instead of letting him have his way with my tenant, I calmed Jason down and assured him he had seen the last of his new chef. So Mr. Potlicker went back to the unemployment office again.

Months later, he figured that working for others was not a good fit for him, so Rodney thought he would try self-employment. Yard care and landscaping would be his next field of endeavor. Our little village actually benefited from his new ambition. When Rodney would overorder sod, flowers, or small trees, he would bring the excess to the mobile home park and distribute the plants in areas that were, until then, barren. The park never looked so good. Things, I thought, were looking up for Mr. Potlicker until I began getting to get calls from local yard-equipment-leasing businesses and landscape sales offices. Rodney was ordering all these plants and rental equipment but was forgetting or neglecting to pay for them. Charges were filed against him, and once again, he was out of work, only this time facing a prison sentence.

With incarceration staring him in the face, Rodney went into deep depression. He and Laura were at each other's throats on a daily basis, and I had to break up many arguments between them. One beautiful spring day, while on our local tennis courts enjoying a friendly game, I got a frantic call from my wife to come home. Rodney apparently had had enough and shot himself in the mouth right in his front yard. By the time I got there, the emergency vehicles had left the scene. The only thing remaining was a pool of blood in the freshly laid sod.

Being a thoughtful landlord, I went to the neighbors who rented down the hill, a couple of old ladies, to inform them of all the commotion. But before I could fill them in, they wanted to tell me of the strange thing they had seen one hour earlier. What they observed was their neighbor Rodney walking around their yard looking up into the branches of a large oak tree.

This, in itself, wasn't what concerned them. What bothered them the most was Rodney was carrying a rope and ladder. Going from tree to tree, he finally gave up and disappeared around the other side of the house. We can only assume the branches he was eyeing were either too high or too low or weren't sturdy enough for his rather extralarge body to hang himself. Instead, he decided to ditch the rope and use a .22 caliber revolver. But just like his other great ideas, he bumbled his own suicide attempt as well.

The gunshot didn't kill him, and after a lengthy stay in the ICU, his wife, Laura, shipped the now totally useless Rodney to his sister's place in Oklahoma. At the same time, she moved in her new boyfriend, and her teen daughter got pregnant. So of course, the baby-daddy/boyfriend had to be added to the lease as well. He only stayed a few weeks until I read in the paper that he followed a waitress home from work late one night and raped her. So off to prison the baby daddy went.

Since no one in the home had a job and she could not pay the rent or utilities, Laura did what anyone would do to survive. She moved her invalid mother in and used Mom's Social Security money to pay for their needs. Now the matriarch of the family was in terrible health. A diabetic in advanced stages, she weighed well under one hundred pounds and was bedridden. Laura wanted nothing to do with her mother other than getting the benefit of the monthly check. After losing one leg to the disease and the impending news of having to remove the other, grandma died and was found by her daughter days after her demise, neglected and rotting in her bed.

To Laura, this meant no more SS checks, so she got a job at the local Ho-Jo. Laura and crew stayed in the home for a few months rent-free until I took her to court and was granted an eviction, a no-trespass order, and garnishment of wages from Ho-Jo. At the rate of what comes from Laura's check every two weeks, it will take three years until her debt will be paid in full. But I say, good riddance to her and her drama.

The perfect ending to this scenario would be for Rodney to recover from his injury—and his luck with this thing we call life—to change for the better.

Coleasing can be one of the worst decisions a landlord can make. First of all, it permits an owner of a trailer to create a business within your business. Also, as landlord, who am I supposed to see when problems arise? And they will. If the rent is not paid on time, do I go to the owner or the coleaser? To whom do I go when a domestic dispute erupts? A sticky wicket will certainly raise its head when a landlord makes the foolish decision of falling into the quagmire of the colease.

Our first encounter of this actually took several years to evolve. Toni J. was a cute, young, single girl, who wanted to move from under the wings of her parents. She purchased an old, beat-up mobile home and moved it into our park. Upon arrival, Toni began to revitalize the fixer-upper by painting the outside of the home and coating the roof. She took on these projects by herself, wearing the shortest cutoffs I have ever seen. During her work details, I would be sure to pass by slowly and ogle on a regular basis just to see how Toni was doing.

With the exterior renovation complete, Toni moved to the interior work. (I missed the cutoffs.) When Toni felt like the home was habitable, she moved in. A short time later, to help with the lot rent, she found a roommate and moved her in as well. Not that it made any difference, but the girl who moved in with Toni was huge and had the biggest human head I have ever seen. She would be driving down the road, and all you could see in the cab of her car was her very large head.

Anyway, the two of them did well as tenants for over a year until Toni met a nice young man. Scott C. was the brother of a friend of mine who had crashed his plane into some nearby mountains and died two years earlier. Toni and Scott fell in love, moved big head out, and made number 13 their little love nest. After several years, wedding bells rang. The two got hitched and bought a house. Not living in the trailer anymore, Toni and Scott asked if they could let some friends colease. I had some initial concerns, but they promised everything would be all right.

Right away things turned bad with the new residents. I don't remember the names of these two scumbags, but I'm sure they weren't friends of Toni and Scott. The male half of the pair was a tattoo-covered, three-time felon, who had done hard time in the penitentiary, and she was a troublemaking, drunken hellcat.

The first nice spring day after their arrival, while I was cutting their yard, my mower hit something hard. Upon inspection, I found a WWI bayonet with mower blade marks on it. Being positive the knife was not there the last time I cut the grass, I asked the female half of number 13 if she knew anything about it. Her reply was, "Yeah, I threw it at him!"

I made a mental note to keep an eye on these two. This was easy to do because neither of them had a job, so they spent all their time terrorizing others in the park and fishing in my pond. Now I raised these fish from fingerlings and fed them each day. I considered them to be my pets, so I asked Mr. Scumbag to catch and release. He assured me he would, but I know each day a bucket of my pets went home to space number 13 to be fried up in cornmeal for their dinner.

I had many other encounters with the two knuckleheads but never mentioned the trouble I was having to the trailer owners and newlyweds, Toni and Scott. After all, I am the cop of the park. Truth be known, these two jerks were the reason I purchased…and still carry…a .38 caliber revolver and enrolled in a martial arts class.

After one particular incident involving an overturned BBQ grill on the front porch of number 13, catching said porch on fire, I decided to inform Toni and Scott of the escapades of their renter friends. They said they had no idea their tenants were being so much trouble and would handle it. When they confronted the idiot renters, Toni and Scott found a full-size, chopped-up motorcycle in the living room of their ex-love nest. We came to an immediate agreement the colease wasn't working for anyone but the troublemakers. We gave them a thirty-day notice to quit, and I gave Toni and Scott sixty days to sell or get rid of the home. News of the eviction did not sit well with the offenders. But being on probation, being on parole, or having warrants, the jailbirds left without much fanfare. I ended up buying the home from Toni and Scott and adding it to my stable of rentals.

No more coleasing for me. It became rule number 1 on my leases, and I have found it eliminates the middleman.

CHAPTER 5

Vacations

One would think being in this line of work creates a certain amount of stress. (One would be correct.) Vacations can be a good way of relieving pressure. Like my wife says, "A getaway can cleanse the body and soul." She should know as she travels more than any one person on the planet and appears to be stress-free.

One of my all-time stress-reducing destinations is a three-day, two-night hike in northern Arkansas. My karate instructor introduced me to this area of canyoneering in the late 1970s, and for a quick getaway, I go there when I can. A variety of people have come on this trip with me. Few have made it a second time.

Beech Creek is a rugged, narrow drainage and tributary to the Buffalo River. The eight-mile hike takes three days due to the myriad amount of bushwhacking, boulder hopping, and creek wading, which one must overcome. I just love it, but it's not for everyone.

A local lady, Euldeene Clark, is usually available to shuttle me and my guest hiker to the top of Cave Mountain. Ms. Clark is the retired post mistress of the area and knows everyone and everything that transpires in the Boxley Valley. She was the first person who told me about the colony of lesbians living on the mountain.

Buffy Sassafras was the matriarch of the community, and I was told to steer clear of her and her following. Apparently, they didn't like men in any way, shape, or fashion—period. My first encounter with Ms. Buffy happened on a trip I took with my father. (Sorry, Dad.) The area had received a good amount of rain at that time, and the creek, which is usually dry in the fall, was overflowing its banks. This created a problem for Dad and me because the creek bed was the easiest way to navigate the canyon. The only way to get from point A to point B was to stay high and dry. This meant much more bushwhacking than normal.

On the second day of our adventure, around noon, we heard barking dogs, and a bit later, we saw a building in the distance. We had no choice but to go onward, so we headed toward the house. When we were closer to the structure, we heard an angry voice say, "Who the hell are you, and what do you want?" A scrawny, unkempt, dark-haired young woman with bad dental care emerged from the doorway with a shotgun. I knew at once, from Euldeene's description of her, this was Buffy.

I tried to assure her we meant no harm and were just passing through. Feeling the 12-gauge pointed at the back of my head, I told my father to keep walking. We proceeded on with great haste and escaped the wrath of Ms. Sassafras. (Keep in mind we were doing this for stress relief.) On the third day of the hike, Dad and I eventually made it back to our truck and drove home safe and sound.

A couple of years later, I invited a friend of mine to attempt the Beech Creek hike. Dr. Martien C. is a PhD-level psychologist and national champion in the art of judo. Since he was strong in mind and body, I figured he would have no problem with the strenuous hike.

The first day was beautiful, with temperatures holding in the sixties all weekend. Ms. Clark dropped us at the church on the mountain, and we traversed down the slope to Beech Creek. The first night was uneventful except for the bobcat circling our camp just on the edge of our firelight.

The next day…déjà vu slapped me in the face. Around noon, the sound of dogs barking led me to believe we were in "Buffy country." Walking a few steps farther down the drainage, we saw clothing hanging from the tree branches. A closer look revealed Ms. Buffy—in the buff—with another young lady beneath her. The dogs' barking alerted the hillbilly homosexuals of our intrusion. Waiting with our backs to them while they got dressed, Ms. Sassafras hurled obscene language at us about trespassing on her property. The more she screamed, the greater the dogs got riled with us.

Looking back, neither Martien nor I could accurately say how many canines were present. I estimated at least half a dozen, and all of them were big, bad, and as mad as their bitch owner. When one of the dogs approached nearer and looked like it was going to have me for a snack, I pulled out my .38 caliber revolver and cranked back the hammer. At the same time, Martien was squirting pepper spray in the dogs' direction. His problem was that the wind was blowing the irritating concoction right back at him.

Seeing the gun and the spray dispenser only infuriated the maniac matriarch even more. She screamed, "Nobody pulls a gun on me on my property!" I calmly told her if she couldn't control her dogs and herself, I was going to start shooting. She cooled down enough to enable Martien and I to walk backward across the creek, our eyes glued on the pissed-off pups.

When we were finally out of sight of the diesel dyke, her gal pal, and the dogs, I looked at Martien and saw him suffering the effect of the irritating spray. With a puffy face, swollen red eyes, and tears rolling down his cheeks, Martien stated he was glad he didn't have the gun because he would have "shot the bitch." (Remember, this is coming from a doctor of psychology.)

All in all, we figured we had one hell of an adventure. The entire week of our return home was filled with nothing but massages and yoga classes, which are also excellent ways to relieve stress.

One other victim—I mean, guest—who I invited to go on the Beech Creek hike, was Bob C., who had been a longtime hiking buddy when he was living in Arkansas.

As usual, Euldeene got us to the church on the mountain, and off we went on a typical three-day, two-night excursion. The weather was great. The hiking was fun and challenging, and Dame Fortune was smiling on us because we did not have an encounter with Ms. Buffy and her maniac mongrels. The entire outing was going very smoothly.

Well, maybe the outing was running a little *too* smoothly... especially for Bob.

I can remember the second morning of our trip, camped in the exact area of the Buffy incident with Martien, peering out of my tent to see a strange sight: Bob was throwing a large article of clothing on the fire. When I asked him what he was doing, Bob replied, "Burning my pants."

Without asking him why and never one to pass up an opportunity, I promptly crawled from my tent and threw my old tennis shoes on the fire. My reason was that the shoes were old and smelly, and I didn't want to carry them on the last day of the hike.

But I think the reason for Bob burning his pants had something to do with the freeze-dried chicken tetrazzini we had eaten for dinner the night before and his not being able to get out of his tent fast enough to, well... (You fill in the blank.)

Note for future hikes: It's probably wise *not* to take rich or spicy foods that might lead to gastrointestinal issues. Stick to the basics!

South Central Utah is another favorite destination of mine for stress relief. Twice each year, I book trips to visit the aforementioned Bob C., who had retired to canyon country (sometime after the Beech Creek event) and taken up residence in the very small town of Escalante. Bob was responsible for introducing me to the strange and wonderful topography of Utah when we began to ride mountain bikes in and around the Moab area in the late 1980s.

June and November are the ideal times of the year, weather-wise, to explore the slot canyons of Utah. Bob always has an exciting adventure destination chosen for us when I get there. Two-, three-, and four-day treks along with day hikes get us into the wild and often unseen wilderness. Not only hiking but also climbing, rappelling, swimming, and fishing have been included in our adventures. Each of these things by themselves would be great, but when you add the awesome scenery of the area and finding Indian pictographs, it makes for a wonderful escapade.

Some of my favorite exploits include Sand and Calf Creeks, Death Hollow, Coyote Gulch, and Water Canyon. Nick S., a neighbor and friend of Bob's, is also a guide in the area. We usually hire Nick for two days of touring while I'm there. The name Water Canyon should have been a clue to the type of adventure on which we were about to embark.

Nick had researched the six-mile drainage by using the topographical map and Google Earth. He determined it was quite possible that no one had ever explored this canyon. Nick came to this conclusion because of its remoteness and the 250-foot free rappel we had to execute in order to get everyone to the head of the chasm. One at a time, we dropped into the bowels of Water Canyon. When the three of us were at the base of the abyss, we retrieved the rope, thinking we would need it further down the drainage. In doing so, we eliminated any hope of escape should the canyon be blocked and we needed to retreat.

The water seeping from the bottom of the cliff and forming a small creek was of no concern to us at that time. About a half mile into the trek, the canyon narrowed into a slot. Normally I love a tight-slot canyon, but this one was deep, with cold spring water. In the heat of summer, this wouldn't be a problem, but during the cooler temperatures of November, hypothermia could be an issue.

A quick assessment was made, and the group's decision was to start climbing. Around noon, we made it to the base of the cliff.

Nick found a crack, which he thought was doable, and I found one I thought I could climb, which was about two hundred feet away. Using all our collective skills, we tried for about four hours to climb each of the cracks. Both potential escape routes proved impossible.

So there we huddled on the ledge like a three-man football team and discussed our predicament. We were two hundred feet down from the top, fifty feet off the ravine floor, and on a cliff ledge measuring about ten feet by ten feet. (Please remember, we were dressed only in gear that would accommodate sixty-degree weather because that was temperature when we started.) We figured a six-mile hike would take about four or five hours to complete. I saw the writing on the wall and immediately began building a rock shelter on a four-by-eight ledge just below.

Now Nick, being the good guide he is, was carrying a spot beacon, which is a GPS sender that can emit our exact location to emergency responders. I had been begging him for hours to push the button because we were stuck and I had to catch a plane the next day. Finally, one hour before dark, the button was pushed and the beacon was sending out our location. (Nick finally had admitted we were screwed.)

About thirty minutes later, we heard the engine of a small plane. Sure enough, a spotter plane was coming up the canyon. Flying low and into the setting sun, the pilot couldn't see us on his first pass. On the next flyby, we flashed our strobe flashlights at him; success, he saw us! Sounding a blare from the siren on his plane, the pilot confirmed that he had our location, and help would soon be on the way!

With the sun setting and temperatures dropping, we started gathering brush and sticks for a fire. At the same time, I was lining my rock shelter with clumps of dried grass to block the wind. Two hours later and well after dark, we heard voices from the top of the cliff. I hollered at them asking if they had a rope (always the optimist). The answer was no but that the rescue team would be here in thirty minutes.

Another two hours later, we heard more voices. The team had arrived, but I didn't want to hear the bad news they had for us: they weren't going to get us out that evening. There was no way I was going to catch my flight departing from Las Vegas the next day. It became obvious that we were spending the night on the ledges. It was too dark for the rescue team to set up a safe rope system to extract us from our situation. They *were* able to send down a goody bag with radio walkie-talkies and more important, space blankets and two hoodies. Grabbing one of the hoodies and a space blanket, I descended to my rock dwelling and attempted to make it through the night.

The temperatures dropped into the twenties. I did wake up one time in the night with bone-shaking shivers, and another time I was awakened by a four-legged visitor. At daybreak, I described the unexpected visitor to Nick, and he said it was probably a ring-tailed cat. Twice, the wild feline had stood on its hind legs and peered over the top of my rock-wall fortress. I can only guess it was trying to see what all the shivering was about.

So everyone made it to see the sun pierce the darkness and light the eastern sky. It was 9:00 a.m. when we heard the first sounds of our rescuers. Through radio contact, they told us it would take about an hour to get the elaborate tripod and rope pulley system in place, which would hoist us to safety.

Around ten o'clock, I tied myself in a double-rope belay system (it was very safe) as the team pulled me up. I was the first to literally walk straight up the cliff wall, two hundred feet, emerging on top. Being greeted by fifteen men and one woman—all members of the rescue team—they were quite a sight. They were led by a guy named Shawn and were very professional, with everyone doing their assigned tasks.

The local sheriff, a team member, asked if I was okay. He was concerned about the blood-soaked bandage he spotted wrapped around my forearm. I assured him I was fine, but in truth, I could have used stitches if we had been rescued a day earlier. I had received a nasty five-inch cut from a rock while trying to climb out, and it has left a great scar on my forearm. (Chicks dig scars.)

Bob was the next on the pulley, and lastly, Nick was retrieved. Did I mention Nick is pushing three hundred pounds and is also a member of the rescue team? I had to help pull him up. He did seem a bit embarrassed when the rest of his team saw who they were rescuing. Everyone made it safe and sound with no charge from the search-and-rescue team. They used it as training mission because none of the members had ever been part of an elaborate rescue like this one.

We three amigos gave our thanks and went on our way. I had spent twenty-two hours on a cliff ledge and made it home a day later than planned. It's amazing the things we do to relieve the stress in our lives.

Okay, so the last several vacation getaways I've described did not end as well as they might have. Hearing two tennis buddies, John and Bud, talking about an upcoming August fishing trip to Canada interested me very much. Lord knows I deserved a nice, peaceful, relaxing, and stress-free retreat. I told them if they could make room for me, I would love to go with them. Another guy, Jerry, was already on board, so it would be the four of us on the twenty-four-hour drive to Canada.

The chosen vehicle was John's mini SUV. Compared to me, the other three guys were huge men, so I was very skeptical about the comfort factor while traveling, especially with the amount of gear we brought. The morning of our departure, Jerry, John, Bud, and I crammed everything and ourselves into the vehicle and started our trek. We were to meet with Bud's daughter, Mary, and her husband, Danny, so there would be a total of six members in the expedition.

After twenty-four hours of driving, we spent the night in a cabin in Crain Lake, Minnesota, just south of the Canadian border. I say we spent the night because there wasn't much *sleep* happening. The three of us discovered that John was a world-class snorer. No kidding, this guy was shaking the glass in the windowpanes. Anyway, the next morning, we met with the outfitter and loaded our gear in his boat (which was a substantial amount according to the guide; he said he had never seen so much crap!).

So off we started on our international adventure, traveling a couple of hours and passing through several lakes. We did three elaborate portages over land on a very old rail system. The portages were achieved by a cradle grabbing the boat from underneath. Then an electrically generated pulley system would hoist the boat up the rails, over the hill, and deposit it in the next lake. Very cool! A bit later, we were pulling up to our homes for the week. After dropping Bud's kids at their cabin, about a mile up lake, we made it to ours.

The place was just beautiful. Exactly what the doctor ordered. Arriving at our dock, up a gentle slope and nestled in the trees was our dream fish camp. With everyone choosing his sleeping quarters, I, being the youngest, took the loft at the top of a winding staircase. After settling in and having supper, we decided to turn in early, with the anticipation of a great day of fishing ahead.

Early on, I knew sleeping was going to be impossible, with the chain-saw-like sounds blaring from John's room. Halfway through the night, in addition to the nighttime noises of John, I heard a rustling in the loft. Grabbing my flashlight and scanning the area, I focused on a mouse tearing into my bag of trail mix. Tossing a pair of underwear at him, I watched the little bastard as he escaped down the stair rail to the lower level of the cabin.

The next morning, after breakfast, we were all eager to explore Lac Lacroix and pursue the aquatic game of the lake. Our landlord, Robert, who lives on the nearby Indian reservation, left us three boats to use. We divided up in pairs, and right away, the competition of catching the largest fish began. Bud and I, the duos of Jerry and John, and Mary and Danny, headed in different directions to see what the lake had to offer. Lac Lacroix is slam full of smallmouth bass, has a good deal of walleye, and, of course, northern pike. I was in heaven, catching several four-pound brownies (smallmouth) and a few in the five-pound range. When the group of anglers gathered at the cabin at the end of the day, each of us shared stories of the large quantities of fish we had caught.

That night, tucked away in my loft with the feeling of total contentment, nothing could keep me from a good night's sleep. Then began the blaring reverberation of the sleeping John. Sometime after midnight, as I was just about to enter la-la land, I felt the presence of another living thing in bed with me. A mouse was crawling on my arm toward my hand. When it reached my palm, I flung the rodent out of the loft and down to the lower dining area. Something had to be done with these pests.

The next day, I located three mousetraps and loaded them with peanut butter. In the next five days, I killed nine of the furry rascals. We were infested! Each morning, we would take the dead vermin down to the lakefront and toss them into the water. Within thirty minutes, an eagle would show up, swoop down, and snatch them into its powerful talons. The majestic bird would then fly into a tall pine tree, right in front of our cabin, and have his breakfast. (I just love this stuff!)

After our breakfast on the second day in Canada, Bud and I decided to head to some waterfalls to try our luck and boat some walleye. Arriving at the falls, I soon began catching some very respectable smallmouth. Bud said he wanted to take some pictures of the lake atop the falls. I was totally happy staying in the area of the lower falls, snagging the fierce-fighting brownies.

This was my utopia. It was a gorgeous day, with perfect weather and a fantastic background of trees and rushing water. The falls were terraced with about a two-hundred-foot drop in total. Each terrace formed a natural pool with hordes of hungry fish in each one. I was working my way through the pools, catching my favorite fish in each one, and was in a pool about halfway to the top of the falls.

That's when I heard the sound of a boat motor. Turning around, I expected to see my friends Jerry and John—after all, we were out in the middle of nowhere—so who else could it be? But it wasn't them.

What I did see were two dark-skinned, dark-haired young men. One was wearing only pajama bottoms, and both were clutching pints of whiskey. When they got out of their boat and started to make their way across the lower falls in the direction of our boat, I knew something was awry. The fast current proved to be too much for them, so they waded back to their boat, got in, and circled—in a beeline—for our vessel. I made my way back to our boat as fast I could, and the three of us arrived at the beached craft at the same time.

Immediately, I began with some friendly small talk and smiles. They did not return the niceties. That's when the tall, drunk Indian with the PJs pointed at our boat and said, "This is my boat," and the other guy actually got in it and sat down. I knew I was in for some trouble. We went round and round for a while with me explaining we were just visiting and were renting the boat and cabin from Robert. I asked if they knew Robert, and they said that they did, but this was their boat, and they were going to take it.

Then things got a bit crazy, with PJ man saying that they were "conservation officers," and he wanted to see my papers. (Actually he said *conversation* officers.) I lied to him, saying my friend had all the papers and that he would be right back, but I have always wanted to meet a "conversation officer" and said, "Let me see *your* identification."

That's when the crazy level intensified, and I began to feel very uncomfortable. The guy in the boat, seated right next to my backpack containing $1,500 worth of travel cash, said, "We are here to bless the waters. We dangle our balls in the water, and it is blessed." (Where in the hell is Bud? He had been gone for an hour. I thought, *Just scalp me now.* But then I remembered I shaved my head.) The whole time this was going on, I had my hands on the gunnel of the boat because there was a canoe paddle just below, six inches from my reach. When PJ man started talking about kidnapping, ransoming, and wanting to see bush, I came very close to going apeshit on him with the paddle.

Lucky for him, he decided to quit harassing me and to go look for my friend, Bud. Minutes later, Bud made his way out of the woods, returning from his photoshoot. The seated, drunk Indian saw Bud and said softly, "He is just an old man. We could take him." Being the outgoing, friendly Southern gentleman he is, Bud walked up and started trying to get acquainted with my new friend. I quickly coaxed the inebriated Native American out of our boat and got Bud in.

We left the falls with great haste with me explaining the horrible situation I had just been through. I was hoping we had seen the last of the native numbskulls. We both tried to shake off the terrible experience by catching some more fish, but what had just occurred was very hard to get your head around, and the feeling of being threatened was hard to shake.

A couple of hours later, Bud and I decided to check on Mary, who was at her cabin by herself. When we got within sight, we could see a boat at the dock, which was not one we had rented. I immediately recognized it as the one belonging to the damn troublemakers. Pulling up to the dock at Mach speed, we saw Mary hustling down the ramp toward us with a frantic look on her face. The idiot Indians had been there for over thirty minutes, harassing her.

Now Mary is the tough, solid, strong-willed Southern-bred daughter of my large friend, Bud, and hunts alligators with her husband for Pete's sake. I have no doubt if it came down to it, she could have turned these two jerks into a couple piles of Native American hamburger. But coming to their rescue in the nick of time saved them from this fate.

So Bud and I grabbed each of the young lads by the nape of the neck and escorted them into their boat. We told them the havoc they had created that day was totally uncool and to take their drunk butts home to the reservation and not to come back.

The next day we told our landlord, Robert, about the events of the previous day. Robert is on the tribal police force and actually was familiar with the offenders because of previous mischief they had gotten into. Robert deeply apologized for all the mayhem created by the two assholes and made a promise to us—we had seen the last of them. He said his extralarge, muscle-bound son would be more than happy to show the two boys the error of their ways. I'm not sure what Robert meant by this, but I am confident no other foreign fishermen visiting the area of Lac Lacroix will be harassed the way we had been.

Mexico can be a wonderful place to go for rest and relaxation. My wife and I travel there each year in January and meet up with friends and family. We always book five-star hotels, which are all inclusive and usually adult only. There is really no need to leave the campus because everything you could want is within the confines of the resort. Wonderful restaurants, multiple pools, activities such as snorkeling, sailing, wall climbing, and shows in the evening can fill a day with much fun and enjoyment. Of course, one can choose to lie around the pool or beach and be attended to, from 10:00 a.m.

to 5:00 p.m., by lovely young Mexican girls, who will bring you the drink of your choice.

"Piña colada, por favor!"

But being the active person I am, I always choose to do at least one high-adventure activity per day. These are the same activities that end up biting me in the ass.

Our first trip south of the border was to Huatulco in southwestern Mexico. My wife's eldest brother was getting married, and we joined fifty members of family and friends to attend. The wedding was beautiful, held on the beach in the early evening, just as the sun was setting into the calm ocean. The entire week was great with warm, tropical weather, good food, fun with friends and family, and, of course, my daily high-adventure activity. Each morning at breakfast, people would ask, "So, Gary, what's it going to be today? Scuba, zip line, fishing, four-wheeling, or river rafting?" And I did them all on that trip.

The week went by very fast, and on the final day, I chose windsurfing as my adventure of the day. This was an unfamiliar sport to me, so I had to teach myself. I had sailed a boat, and I am a snowboarder, so I used those skills to figure out how to put together sailing while standing on a surfboard.

After thirty minutes, I thought I had the hang of it when suddenly I was hit by a gust of wind. There I was, falling backward off the board into the water, then swimming to the surface only to be smashed square in the face by the boom. Shaking the cobwebs off, I noticed that the water all around me was turning pink in color. Just great, now all that I could think of was *shark*! Climbing back on the board, I paddled to shore to the gathering crowd, who had been watching my pathetic first attempt at windsurfing.

Off to the doctor I was hustled for medical attention. The next day, I boarded the plane for home with stitches, a broken nose, and two black eyes.

On a subsequent trip to Mexico, we visited the beautiful city of Puerto Vallarta. We just love it, and this destination has probably turned out to be our favorite.

Now I was at the time very involved in the sport of mountain biking, so I looked up a local bike shop from which to rent a bike. The owner, Oscar, could tell I wasn't just a la-de-da peddler when he saw I had my own helmet, shoes, padded shorts, and gloves. Oscar set me up with a guide so I wouldn't get lost in the trails of the jungle. We decided on a route named Killer Donkey, which was an out-and-back ride.

The first fifteen miles were all up, which meant the second half was all down. The ride out of town to the turnaround was grueling, going straight up the mountain. We also have mountains in Arkansas, so I was fine. At the farthest part of our ride, we had lunch at a little Mexican lady's house, where she prepared beans and tortillas for us.

On the way back down the mountain, I decided to test the skills of my guide. We were probably hitting speeds of thirty to forty miles per hour on the dirt double track. I pulled ahead of him just in time to hit a very loose, crazy-sharp corner. The front tire washed out from under the bike, slamming me to the ground. When my body stopped skidding in the gravel, I took inventory, like I always do after a bad wreck, finding I had taken skin off down to the bone. To this day, I'm very proud to show off the scars I earned in Mexico. (I think I mentioned, "Chicks dig scars!")

The most memorable high-adventure incident happened on our first trip to Ixtapa. This was to be our twenty-fifth wedding anniversary gift to ourselves, and we were very excited. Our room was on the fifth floor of the resort, and we decided when we got there, we were not going to use the elevator (always keeping fitness in mind).

Gay was up early and went to breakfast, with me minutes behind. When I got to the bottom of the stairs, a large group had gathered around a crumpled Gay. She had fallen down the last flight of stairs and broken her foot. When the house doctor was called, we found out he wasn't going to make it to the resort until after noon. So I found the only wheelchair on the premises and rolled Ms. Gay to breakfast.

So we decided since the doctor was delayed, we would leave the campus to swim with the dolphins, something we always wanted to do. We managed to catch a cab, loaded the chair, and headed to the dolphins. When we got to the pool with the sleek gray mammals, I rolled Gay up to the pool's edge and dumped her in. It was quite amazing being in the water with the large creatures. They were very strong, pulling us around the pool, but seemed to take great care not to hurt or bump the injured foot of my spouse. We really believe the dolphins could sense Gay was in pain. When we were finished with Flipper, the cab returned us to our resort. The doctor had still not arrived.

It was at that time I noticed people in the ocean bodysurfing. Always wanting to try something new, I told Gay to wait at the pool for the doctor, and I would be back soon. Now this was fun; the waves did all the work. Just swim out a bit and then let the wave push you all the way to the beach. There were probably ten of us taking advantage of the hydroride, each taking turns in the moving surf.

When a particularly large wave formed in the distance, I noticed that everyone was steering clear of it. I, on the other hand, thought this was the one I had been waiting for. Swimming with reckless abandon toward the beach, I caught the rogue wave and began my ride. About halfway in, the wave picked me up, perpendicular to the hard-packed sandy bottom and hammered me face-first into it.

Being deposited about twenty feet from shore, I gathered my wits and discovered I had no movement in my arms. I managed to stand and stagger to the water's edge before anyone noticed the bloody-faced man with limp arms. Hotel guests escorted me to find my wife by the pool at the same time the doctor got there. I said, "Doctor, we have been waiting for you to look at my wife's foot." He said he was going to look me over first. By the time, he loaded us both into a resort van, the use of my arms had come back.

The doctor said we were headed to a clinic for X-rays. When we got to the clinic, we noticed the waiting room was full of dogs, cats, and a pig. It was a veterinarian clinic with an X-ray machine. When we got our results, we found that Gay had indeed broken her foot, and I had a broken vertebra in my neck.

Valuable lessons were learned: leave tsunami-sized waves alone, and make good use of all available elevators.

For the rest of the week, I had to push my wife around the resort in a wheelchair. One night, the chair was not to be found. Being the resourceful husband that I am, I located a two-wheeled dolly from maintenance. Gay was rolled to dinner in style, wearing her formal evening gown and cast, with me wearing a cervical collar. Both of us were covered head to foot with flea bites we received at the vet clinic. Needless to say, we really got the looks. Many folks asked us what kind of wreck we had been in.

Years later, we scheduled another trip to Ixtapa so we could properly celebrate our twenty-fifth anniversary without mishap.

CHAPTER 6

Bad People

Bad people come in all sizes, shapes, nationalities, colors, and genders.

One particularly awful person was a very large, dark-skinned Afro-American female by the name of Shaniqua Washington. During her initial application interview, Shaniqua said she was a single mother with three children, saying, "I gotsta have me a three-betroom troiler." I agreed to rent her a nice "three-betroom, two-bath," which included a washer/dryer, dishwasher, central heat and air, storage building, and carport.

It wasn't long before I noticed what seemed to be a dozen unfamiliar, dark young faces running around, terrorizing the trailer park. When the complaints started rolling in, I "axed" Shaniqua about all the additional children; she said she was watching some of her sister's kids. I decided to let it slide, not wanting to start an all-out racial war with Ms. Washington.

Soon I began getting calls from her about stupid things like a light bulb is out, her car ran out of gas, dogs got in her garbage, the kids heard a snake in the vent hood above the stove, "My table leg fell off," "I can't find my keys," "I can't find my glasses," and "My car battery is dead." The calls came almost on a daily basis to the point where I felt like I was Shaniqua's personal rent-a-husband. Each time I would promptly take care of the situation, with no thanks or acknowledgment.

Whenever I came into the home to fix something, I could see three to four children in each room, and there was always a strange man lying in the bed of the master betroom. When I asked about the guy, all I got was, "Yo just never minds who dat is in my betroom!" The house was a disaster, with the kitchen being the most deplorable area. Grease covered everything. I suppose preparing large quantities of "soul food" will do that.

Complaints from tenants got worse about the mob in number 28, but when an allegation of drug activity came to my attention, I figured it was time to have it out with Shaniqua. She couldn't come up with a good excuse for the high volume of traffic day and night. I "axed" her why she had been seen placing packets of something on the left front tire of her car. Minutes later, a stranger drove in and parked next to her car and retrieved the object, leaving another package. I never got a good explanation of what was happening. (This apparently occurred many times according to my confidential informant.) What I did get was a scathing tongue-lashing from Shaniqua, saying, "If'in you don't minds your own damn bidness, I'll get my bros on you." First of all, I thought this *was* my "bidness," and second, her brothers would have a hard time getting me because they were already in jail with charges of a multiple homicide.

The straw that broke this camel's back was the day Shaniqua came to me, "axing" for gas money to get to work. (She didn't work and received several government checks each month, probably one check per child.) I gave her a $10 bill and set my brilliant plan into action by stealthily following her and boyfriend to the "gas station." Turning into a liquor store parking lot, I surprised them by pulling in behind. When boyfriend pulled a gun on me and said to get the f—— out of his face, I decided I had enough of the lovely Shaniqua and her basketball team. (She actually had seven kids.)

Finding the ten-day notice to quit posted on her door when she got home, Shaniqua went ballistic. She remained in that condition for the next three months until a judge issued the eviction order, and the sheriff's department escorted her out. The place was left in such a horrible condition I thought I might just have to burn it. But after several months and hundreds of dollars later, the renovation was complete, and I rented number 28 again.

One year later, I read in the paper that the bros of Shaniqua got out of the murder rap and were free to kill again. It seems the witnesses who were to testify against them had disappeared. This was just another reason for me packing heat and watching my back.

One day, another horribly bad person showed up at my door, wanting to rent a trailer with her equally horrible boyfriend. First, some background information. In late summer, I had rented a small two-bedroom to Brian and his daughter Angie, a soon-to-be-of-age seventeen-year-old. Having a highly developed eye for trouble, I figured by the looks of these two, they deserved to be watched closely. The pair came without a vehicle (*red flag!*), and Brian had a patch over his left eye, which I never understood because he only wore it every other day. (Maybe he wanted to be a pirate.) I asked if they would need any help moving in, but Brian told me his parents lived right down the street, and they would be helping him and Angie.

The first two months went by without incident. That's when Brian informed me he wanted a larger and nicer home to raise his young daughter. Unit number 6 had just been vacated, and I figured it was what Brian was looking for. The two inspected unit number 6 and fell in love with it. Not having any resources (his parents had doctors' appointments that day), Brian asked if I could help him move his possessions into the new residence. I grabbed my handyman and yard guy to help load all the stuff onto my flatbed trailer, and we relocated Brian, his daughter, and their junk. Brian wasn't any help because of the recent surgery and cast on his hand, where he had a pin inserted, due to a tree-punching incident. (I didn't ask.)

Two months passed with no major episodes. Then Brian told me his parents were interested in moving into the park. He said they would need a three-bedroom home because they were raising two grandchildren belonging to his sister, Anna, who was a "horrible person." (His words, not mine.)

At our initial application interview, Mr. and Mrs. Feebleton seemed truly nice but very timid. They reminded me of a couple of mice, which had been chased around by hungry cats for the last twenty-five to thirty years. Of course, this was the approximate ages of Brian and his sister, Anna. One could only guess the terrible and horrifying situations these poor people had been through with their bad seeds. So once again I recruited my onsite helpers and, four trailer loads later, relocated the family to unit number 28.

Once again, Brian was of no help, this time wearing a back brace after a fall off the couch while reaching for a beer bottle. (This guy was the Les Nessman of the trailer park.) Anyway, a couple months went by before I started to notice the screen on Angie's bedroom window was out of the frame and on the ground. Each time I would find it this way, I'd put it back in place. It was explained to me by Father Brian that his little girl was sneaking out late at night, pulling train for a bunch of young men at another trailer park down the street. (It's this kind of stuff that greatly reinforces my decision not to have children.) When Brian confronted Angie with the situation, she promptly had *him* investigated by DHS for sexual abuse.

During this time, I got to meet Anna, the horrible sister of Brian, and child to Mr. and Mrs. Feebleton. Anna showed up with her boyfriend, coming straight from a court-ordered rehab and looking for a trailer to rent. Everything about her emanated a long-term crack/meth user. She smelled of something unidentifiable, was skin and bone thin with scraggly, dirty hair and only 50 percent of the teeth God had given her. Mr. Boyfriend was in about the same condition as Anna. He limped along with a cane, wore a top hat and a cape, and was twice Anna's height and age.

When I invited them into my home and office, my dog, Ellie, started to go crazy. She began snarling and barking, and the hair on her back was sticking straight up. Now my sweet dog was eight years old and had never in her life acted that way before, but I can't say as I blame her. Anna came busting in all lovey-dovey and huggy, calling me sweetie and honey. My creep-o-meter was going off big time, as was my dog's. I told them to go and look at trailer number 19, and I would be down shortly to let them in.

As soon as they left, I called the senior Feebletons to do a quick background check on their daughter. Explaining their daughter's intentions, my only question was, "Had Anna ever been arrested?" They gave me the answer I had already suspected. Their daughter had been arrested numerous times and had warrants out for her in three states. I hung up the phone and rushed to unit number 19 before they could break in. I met them at the front door with them being anxious to see their potential new flophouse. Blocking their entrance, I turned to ask, "One question, have either of you ever been arrested?"

They looked at each other, then back at me and said, "No!"

I then let them know about the fastest background check I had ever done and told them I knew they were lying. I also told Anna I wasn't her friend or lovey-dovey sweetie and informed her that I was the landlord, and besides, "My dog doesn't like you!" They left with their tails between their legs, and I had dodged a bullet.

Four months later, we read in the paper that Anna had died of a drug-induced heart attack. RIP, Anna, at least you will no longer have to live with the pain of addiction.

How many people can say they have met a narcissistic, lying, psychopathic, deceiving, thieving sociopath? Count me as one that has.

Daniel "Dumber than Dirt" Dumas came to us pleading to rent a two-bedroom trailer. He had a very sad story about how he, his wife, and two children were living in a home infested with poisonous snakes. (I found out later they were being evicted from a very nice apartment owned by a friend of mine.) Believing their terrible story, I felt so bad for them that I let them move in immediately, saying we would work out the details later.

A couple days after the move-in, I came by the unit to get the lease signed and to read them the rules. It was late in the day, and Daniel said they were on their way out to shop for groceries, so I said I would be back the next day. At this point, I was a bit nervous, but helping families in need is what we are all about. Keep in mind, I had not as yet received the rent or deposit from the newbies.

Passing by the unit several times the next day proved to be a waste. There was no one answering the door, and the phone number they gave me was out of service. An uneasy feeling began to grow from within my gut. The next week, I did manage to make contact with Daniel four to five times. Each time he had excuses for not being able to get me any money. The list of reasons included the following: (1) his check from the tire sales office, where he worked, hadn't cleared (he never had worked there); (2) his very large tax return should arrive any day; (3) an even larger insurance check from an accident was past due; (4) he was fired from the nonexistent tire sales job; (5) they were waiting for the return of the deposit from their last residence; and (6) he was expecting $100 bills to come shooting out of his ass (I made that one up).

Realizing I had been had, I issued a ten-day notice to quit. Arguing with me that he deserved a thirty-day notice and not the ten-day, I assured Mr. Dumas the sheriff's department would indeed be in the park to serve him in ten days. Nine days into his notice, I witnessed Daniel and a friend loading his kitchen set into a truck. He told me they were taking the set to an auction so he could get some money for me. On a hunch, after they left, I went into the unit and found it to be completely empty. Not only had they taken all his stuff, but *my* washer/dryer, water heater, refrigerator, stove, and toilet were gone as well. Who would steal a toilet? Oh yeah, Daniel

"Dumber than Dirt" Dumas, the narcissistic, lying, psychopathic, deceiving, thieving sociopath. *That's who!*

Years later, I saw an alert on the TV from law enforcement agencies of Arkansas. Our ex-tenant, Daniel, made it to Arkansas's most wanted. It seems that Mr. Dumas graduated from stealing household items to grand theft auto, assault, and robbery. Congratulations, Daniel "Dumb Ass." You made it to the bigs!

Accepting a renter through the local housing authority means two things. You *will* get the rent on the third of the month, and the tenant signs a one-year lease. Getting the money on a regular basis is great; being stuck with an atrocious renter for one year…not so much.

Normally, I get a six-month signed lease and then go month to month after that time. It's much easier to rid yourself of the offending scumbags if they are on a month-to-month basis.

Rhonda Slobovitch and her two young daughters came to me through HUD. I have helped people through the housing program before with mostly bad results. I figure about 90 percent of the experiences I've had with HUD folks ended negatively. But I keep trying.

The all-female family settled on a small two-bedroom, one-bath mobile home. Rhonda was a student at a local college. I know for a fact that Ms. Slobovitch wasn't studying interior decorating because from the onset of her time with us, her home was a train wreck. After several complaints from me, the condition of the home only got worse. My main concern was for the little girls. Living in that environment had to be very unhealthy.

Dr. Bugg, the bug man, was scheduled to come and spray all my rentals in March of that year, and this would be getting close to Rhonda's six-month anniversary with us. I decided to do a deeper inspection of her home when I went around with Dr. Bugg.

Entering the Slobovitch's residence, the first thing we noticed was the Christmas tree still being up in the corner of the living room, fully decorated. I found this quite strange because Rhonda had signed the lease with me in November of the previous year. Six months later made it April. Wading through the carnage to the kitchen, I opened the refrigerator and was appalled to see the Thanksgiving turkey carcass, rotting on a platter. That's when you could hear the back of the camel crack.

I went home and got the digital camera, came back, and took pictures of all the rooms in the house. When I showed them to the inspector at the Housing Authority, she said she was very sorry their client was treating our property so poorly and would look into the matter.

A week later, I knew Rhonda must have had contact with the inspector from HUD because as I was getting the mail from my box, she made a beeline for me, running over the mailbox with her car and almost making a hood ornament of me. Instead of filing a police report, I contacted HUD again, telling them of my narrow brush with death. Officials of the Housing Authority contacted Ms. Rhonda, informing her she was no longer a part of their program. They even gave her a three-day eviction with a threat of imprisonment if she did not comply. (The government doesn't play around!)

I guess I'll give HUD another chance after all. Lord knows I love that money on the third of each month.

Being in the type of business that we are, trailer park rentals, running into a bad apple is a common occurrence. A fisherman by the name of Big Bad Bill Bullyman was literally the largest bad apple I have ever met. Big Bill stood close to seven feet tall, was very unkempt with long, dirty hair and beard, and smelled of fish, wet dogs, and alcohol, which made sense because he told me that he fed his pack of dogs most of the fish he caught.

Big Bad Bill had been renting a boat stall from another park next door (I didn't know that) and had been asked to leave (I didn't know that either). He had heard that we had an opening and was anxious to rent a stall from us. It was only after he rented the stall from us that I learned of his disinvitation from the neighboring park.

Soon after he brought his boat to our docks, complaints began to come to me about Bill's bad attitude. Frankly, he was a scary person all round. In the beginning the grievances against Bill were minor. "He stinks," "He looked at me funny," and "He parked in my space" were all petty complaints that I could overlook.

But when I found out that Big Bill was cussing others out and actually had started a fight with another fisherman by the name of Gil (his real name), I confronted the very large man. He said that the fight was Gil's fault for fishing in his, Bill's, favorite spot on the lake.

After talking with both parties, I thought things had calmed down. They hadn't. After another assault, Gil told me he was carrying a 12-gauge shotgun with him. He said if that SOB, Bill, got anywhere near him on the lake, he would shoot him right out of his boat.

Attempting to avoid a homicide, I told Bill that when the month was up, he would have to find another place for his boat. He didn't take this well. While leaving the park, he spun the wheels of his truck, throwing gravel at my house and me. Everyone had heard about—and agreed with—my decision to kick Big Bill out. The last days of his time with us came and went without incident.

Well, almost…because Bill hadn't left.

I knew this because our bedroom sat right above the boat dock, and his boat was still in the stall. The first time I saw Bill after noticing this, I confronted him and asked why he was still there. His reply was that he wasn't going *nowhere* and that if I forced the issue, he would "own this place." I went into our house, got a camera, and took pictures for evidence that he was still on the property past the deadline I had given him. After much cussing and verbal abuse from him, what did it for me was when he said, "You don't know how to handle a guy like me."

Well, I sure do! I dialed 911. The sheriff's department came, slapped the cuffs on him, and threw Big Bill into the back of a squad car. Spending some time in jail must have been a very humbling experience for Bill. Every time I ran into him after that, he was apologetic and kind to me. He said that he had never been arrested before (I found *that* hard to believe) and that he didn't ever want to go to jail again.

Peace was once again restored on the waterfront.

CHAPTER 7

Weather

Weather can have a devastating effect on a trailer park, especially the wide variety we see in Arkansas. Straight-line winds, hail, snow, ice, flooding due to torrential downpours, lightning, and the dreaded tornados are all capable of doing large quantities of damage to the structures in which we choose to live. Like I said before, "What do Arkansas divorces and tornados have in common? Somebody's gonna lose a trailer."

The first winter I spent in my new home state proved to be a trying one. The ice storm we experienced that year covered everything with six to eight inches of the frozen liquid. As beautiful as it was, it proved to be devastatingly destructive. Ice is a lot heavier than just plain old snow. Eight inches of the white stuff is never a problem for anyone except those who have never driven in it. Being from Chicago, I actually enjoy plowing my four-wheel drive pickup through deep snow. The big problem one runs into while doing this is all the idiot Southerners with no snow-driving skills. I want to scream at them, "When it snows, JUST STAY HOME!"

But let's go back to my first introduction to ice (in Arkansas… in a trailer park). After the storm blew through, I began to get calls from tenants. The weight of the ice was causing all the awnings in the park to sag, some more than others. Al Hook, the one-armed fisherman, was the first to contact me, saying he thought his awning was going to go down at any moment. He was right!

The instant I tried to pull some of the heavy frozen stuff from atop the awning with a rake, the entire full-length covering came down with a roar. The ladder and I ended up crashing down on top of the mess. Al wasn't as lucky, somehow ending up underneath the aluminum scrap pile. It's a good thing I was a retired gymnast who knew how to fall, and Al was a tough old bird who could take a good lick. Neither Mr. Hook nor I were hurt in the incident, and homeowners' insurance took care of the damage.

The phone calls kept coming from tenants, distressed about their droopy awnings. But after finding out how I handled my first attempt to assist with the problem, most opted to keep me in my house and let the sun aid them by melting the situation away.

Taking a walk around the park to see what other trouble I might find, I noticed our twelve-stall boat dock was about a foot lower in the water than it should be. The boats in the stalls were being dragged down to the point where if they sank any further, they might as well have been submarines. I had to do something.

Gathering up all the tools I thought I would need to break up the ice and push it off into the lake, I headed to the task. Halfway down the path to the dock, my wife yelled out the door and told me to "wear a life jacket!" Who would have thought breaking up an eight-inch sheet of ice on the slippery roof of a boat dock in midwinter would require the use of a life jacket? (I must mention that my wife is the smartest person I know.)

Upon clearing about a third of the roof of its heavy, cold coat, I could tell the dock was floating a bit higher. When I started pushing off the next section, I felt the block of ice—which I was standing on—move. Like riding a snowboard, I was headed for the edge of the dock roof and picking up speed. The next thing I knew, I was in the water with the rest of the floating icebergs. It was then I decided, like the rest of my renters, to wait it out and let the sun do its thing.

Needless to say, ice storms can wreak havoc on trees and overhead power lines. This particular storm was hell on both. Huge jack pine trees were folded over, pulling out entire root wads. Oak branches as big around as my waist broke off and fell to the ground. Each tree that snapped from the weight of the ice sounded like a cannon going off. The electric lines didn't have a chance against all the lumber coming down.

The entire area was without electricity for seventeen days. After the swim in the lake and without a heater, my only problem with no electricity was trying to get dry and regain feeling in my extremities. This was accomplished by standing over the gas stove with all the burners on.

Strong, damaging winds are my worst nemesis and fear. Ice is bad, but the carnage of a straight-line wind, especially with all the trees we have scattered around the trailers, can be very destructive. It's said, trailer parks are magnets for tornados, and that seems to be true. In fact, if any structure is visited by the direct hit of a tornado, it will pretty much be demolished. We have been spared the wrath of the evil, spinning high winds but have experienced some very strong straight lines. One storm, which I will never forget, came and went with a vengeance.

After it passed, Mary Lee from unit number 17 called and said she thought there was a branch down and lying on the porch of unit number 24. When I got to the scene of the downed branch, I found it was actually a huge, one-hundred-plus-year-old pin oak tree on top of the trailer. The family had just left to go shopping before the storm hit. (Thank God.)

Entering the home through the front door, everything was normal in the living room, kitchen, and laundry room. As I walked down the hall and opened the door to the master bedroom, I thought, *Holy crap!* It looked, smelled, and felt like a tropical rain forest. I half-expected to see Jane Goodall sitting in a corner of the room, taking notes while watching a family of mountain apes. The entire room was full of dripping wet pin oak branches. If the renters had been home in bed at the time of the incident, we would have had fatalities because the tree smashed the bed flat to the floor.

After a quick assessment of the situation, I jumped into my tree service and demolition mode. I gathered up tools for the task of cleanup and prepping for the repair of the damaged structure. A chain saw, handsaw, pry bar, ladder, rake, broom, pruning snips, shop-vac, and a large tarp were all I needed to get started. (I love demo.)

After making a call to Phil, my mobile home repair guy, I began to first clear the master bedroom. It was my thought to start there because I didn't want the tenants to freak out after seeing their bedroom in its current deplorable state. Cutting, splitting, and hauling… it was a huge undertaking, but after two hours of nonstop labor, I eventually got all the foliage relocated out of the bedroom and back outside to the yard, where it belonged. Creating an even worse mess from all the wood chips of the chain saw, I spent another hour cleaning the room with a rake, broom, and vacuum cleaner. The inside was looking pretty good except for the squashed bed and gaping hole in the ceiling…but help was on the way.

When Phil, my go-to repair guy, got there, he assessed the damage and then helped me cover the hole with a tarp. Twenty-four hours later, the home was totally repaired with a new metal roof, ceiling fan, and textured ceiling with fresh paint. The bed—I'm sorry to say—didn't make it.

For the next two weeks, I cut up the rest of the gigantic oak into firewood. It is said pin oak is a wood splitter's wet dream, and it does split very easily. It still was a lot of work getting it all cleaned up and toted to the top of the hill to my firewood pile. On the bright side, from this one tree, we had enough firewood to heat our home for the next three winters.

Another weather-related boat dock incident occurred in the middle of the night during one humid July. The National Weather Service had been sending out warnings all day long about the horrible storm, which was to hit our area that night. Boy, did they get it right for a change!

Heeding the warnings, I had prepared my usual emergency nighttime uniform and attempted to get some rest before the storm hit. About 1:00 a.m., I heard the distant rumbling of thunder. Around 1:30 a.m., lightning flashes accompanied the thunder. At 2:00 a.m., wind, rain, lightning, and thunder hit our area with a vengeance. The horizontal winds were strong enough to shake our mobile home to the point where we thought it would be blown off its blocks. I watched through our bedroom window, which faced the lake.

One particular lighting strike, when the winds were at their strongest, caused me to think something looked funny about our boat dock. The next flash proved me right. The dock appeared to be ten feet farther from the shore than it should have been. To my horror, each time the sky lit up, the east side of the dock was farther from the lake's bank until the entire twelve-stall boat dock was *gone*. Vanished in a flash! Gone with the wind! Halfway through the show, I asked my wife if what I was seeing was real. She confirmed that indeed what I was seeing was actually happening.

The next morning was beautiful. The storm had cleansed the air of the usual pollens of July. The yards, on the other hand, were filthy with debris left by the previous night's violent outbreak. Branches, leaves, sticks, and trash from blown-over garbage cans covered the landscape. But all that had to wait.

My first priority of the day was to locate and retrieve the AWOL boat dock. It was about that time the first avid fisherman of the park showed up and asked me, "What did you do with the dock, and where is my boat?" After telling John the story of the events of the previous night, I borrowed a boat from the marina up the bay (I worked there part time) and asked John—of the missing boat—to come with me in search of my dock and his boat.

We jumped into the loaner and headed west down the lake. After one mile of puttering along the shore, I spotted the dock in the cove of an island. The entire flotilla, with all twelve boats, was sitting pretty as you please, nestled in the cove and totally intact. John's boat was on the far left side in stall number 1. I tied the borrowed boat on the outside of the far right of the dock. I then instructed John to get into his boat and push his throttle to half speed. It was clear right away that if I also kept my throttle at half speed, we would go straight. If I pushed it above that, we turned right. In reverse, we would turn left.

We traveled like this all the way back to our lakefront property. Now the boat dock itself is over one hundred feet long, but the way I maneuvered the thing right back to its home was a work of art. A couple of hours later, I had the ramps reconnected and the guide wires tight and tied off. The best thing after that were the cheers and applause from the avid anglers who had been waiting to go out on the lake and test their skills.

Ice, snow, and wind are three of the four forms of weather that can cause problems for a mobile home park. The fourth trouble-maker, weather-wise, would be large hail. I'm not talking about pea-sized hail, which can occur before, during, and after a thunderstorm. Pea-sized hail is a regular form of Arkansas weather. The relatively small ice balls make one hell of a racket falling on the roof of a mobile home. But rarely are they heavy enough to do any damage. Large hail, golf-ball size and bigger, is another matter altogether.

One beautiful, sunny, hot June day suddenly turned for the worse with a severe thunderstorm blowing up out of nowhere. Big black clouds and wind began to build with no warning. Running into our house, a double-wide mobile home, I just made it before the storm cut loose. Watching from our sliding glass doors, the trees began to dance with the strong winds. Then the rain began to join the wind in a horizontal assault.

Minutes later, I heard what sounded like marbles hitting the roof. The hail started in the harmless form of peas but soon grew in size. When golf-ball-sized hail started to fall, I backed away from the glass doors. When balls of solid ice the size of my fist fell, I got under a heavy oak coffee table. Peeking out the door from under the table, I could see that we were going to need new lawn chairs and a new hot tub cover. The now softball-sized hail was going right through both of them along with a canoe I had stored upside down in the yard. The onslaught lasted only a few minutes, but it seemed like hours.

When the storm relented, I went outside to check on the damage and knew it wouldn't be hard to find. Not only were the yard furniture, hot tub cover, and canoe trashed, but the siding, roof shingles, and window screens on our home also had holes everywhere. Our vehicles looked like someone had gone berserk with a ball-peen hammer on the hood, roof, and trunk lid.

Most of the leaves had been ripped from the trees, and there were many dead birds and squirrels lying on the ground. Many ducks were found dead and scattered about on the lake.

All the homes had taken similar hits, and one home actually had hailstones go right through the roof and ceiling, ending up in the living room. I even heard of people getting caught off guard out in the open, who were knocked out and just about beaten to death by the ice bombs.

This was one storm where it would have been nice to have insurance on all my rentals. But who can afford it?

CHAPTER 8

Phone Calls

Inquiries over the phone for rentals or spaces in the mobile home park can be very informing, interesting, amusing, confusing, telling, and sometimes even frightening. Since we don't advertise much, I can only assume most calls originate from folks locating our number in a directory, off the internet, or when driving by and seeing the phone number on our sign at the entrance to the park.

With virtually everyone owning a cell phone (everyone except my first editor, that is), it is quite common to get calls from needy prospective renters, parked at the entrance, wondering what we have for rent. I like handling these calls because they usually accomplish several objectives in the process of choosing a new member for our park family.

How people handle themselves over the phone will give the prospective landlord (me) a first impression. I believe first impressions are very important. Can I hear and understand the caller over the noise coming from the defective muffler, which is falling off their car? Do they have an accent? Can they form sentences? Are they talking with their mouth full? Is English their second language? All these things, when communicating with someone for the first time, can be very telling about the person who is about to drive up the hill to my office.

There have been many times I didn't like the voice or attitude of the inquiring person, so I immediately and untruthfully raised the rent and deposit quote to them or better yet said, "I just rented my last available home one hour ago." Another goal I can mark off the list when receiving a drive-by call is checking out the condition of the vehicle they are driving. Loud, old, banged-up, POS (piece of s———) cars are never a good idea when trying to make a good first impression.

My thought of the *perfect* incoming phone inquiry would go something like this:

> Caller: I was driving by your beautiful mobile home park and saw a sign that says you have something to rent. My wife and I are being relocated to your area due to our jobs, and we are looking for a three-bedroom, two-bath home to raise our two young children. (With these two sentences, my first impression has already gone to a level of ten.)
>
> Me: Do you have any pets? (I like to go to my checklist.)

Caller: No. (Perfect, because I don't permit pets.)

Me: How many vehicles do you have?

Caller: Two, both late-model BMWs. (Be still, my heart.)

Me: How soon do you need to move?

Caller: We aren't in any big hurry, but as soon as possible would be great. We aren't expected at our new positions for three weeks but would like to orient ourselves to the area and get our children enrolled into their new school district. (I want these people!)

Me: I believe I have the perfect three-bedroom, two-bath, double-wide home for you and your family. It goes for $700… I mean $800 per month, with a $500… I mean $600 deposit.

Caller: Sounds nice, but like I said, we are new to the area, and we haven't had time to set up a bank account yet, so all I have is cash.

Me: Cash works for me. Meet me at the top of the hill at my home and office, and I will escort you and your family to your new abode.

If these people are able to find me with the simple directions I have given them, this could be the beginning of a wonderful relationship. Over the phone, in a short time, I have learned this is a young family with both adults employed, nice cars, no pets, no sense of urgency, and they have *cash*!

Keep in mind this is my idea of the perfect call, and I am *still* waiting for it to actually happen.

Now let's look at a sampling of calls I have *actually* fielded over the last four decades.

Caller: Is this the trailer park?

Me: Yes, this is the mobile home village. (It just
    sounds better.)
Caller: What you got for rent?
Me: How many bedrooms do you need, one,
    two, or three? (I like to ask the questions.)
Caller: It's just me and my old lady. (I let the term
    old lady slide and continue.)
Me: Do you have any pets?
Caller: Just two dogs, but I keep 'em in a pen
    outside. (That did it! Wrong answer.)
Me: I'm sorry, but I don't permit pets.
Caller: We never let them in the house.
    Then I have to explain, "Sir, I don't permit
    outside pets because I have residents who
    work at night and sleep during the day." I
    go on to tell him, "I can't have barking dogs
    in the park disturbing my tenants." Then
    come my dreaded words to them, "I'm so
    sorry, I can't help you."
Caller: *Click.*

This call was short and to the point, not wasting much of the caller's time or mine. Now he is free to go elsewhere and locate a place for his old lady and his dog kennel.

Hot Springs, Arkansas, where we live, is also home to the Oaklawn horse racing park. The surrounding area is slam full of stables and horse training centers. During the live racing season, January through April, I am inundated with calls from Spanish-speaking people from south of the border. Apparently, many of these folks are small in stature but very good around the large animals. They are a perfect fit for training, grooming, and hot-walking the beasts after a workout. Many Hispanics become jockeys and do very well traveling the circuit of horse racing. A typical phone call will go something like this.

> Caller: Chew got troiler me rent? (Try to read
> this with a heavy Hispanic accent.)
> Me: How many bedroom? Uno, dos, o tres? (I
> like to practice my Spanish.)
> Caller: Ah, uno o dos.
> Me: How many people, bambinos, brothers,
> seesters, peros? (I like to screw with them.)
> Caller: Tres bambinos y tres peros. (This means
> three children and three dogs.)
> Me: Ah, no peros permiso. Mucho sorry, señor.
> Caller: No peros? Basta! (I don't know what that
> means.)

I really need to brush up on my Spanish.

With all the dealings I have had with people of the homosexual variety, I am becoming quite the gay and lesbian specialist. I've gotten to the point to where I almost feel like a lesbian magnet.

After going through the introduction and application process with what I suspected to be a female couple, I rented unit number 29 to Tiffany and Joe. The former was a large but not unattractive black woman, and her partner, Joe, who looked like a thirteen-year-old boy, was definitely the butch of the two. Since the girls moved in on the fifteenth of February, I prorated the first month's rent in half, explaining to them that their first full month's rent would be due on March 1. The following are examples of calls I received from them in the initial three weeks of staying with us.

> Tiffany: Mr. Gary, we lost our mailbox key. (This
> is really no problem because I keep spare
> keys.)
> Tiffany: Mr. Gary, we locked ourselves out. (Not
> a problem; I let them back in the house.)
> Joe: Mr. Gary, we lost our mailbox key. (I explain
> that I have given another key to Tiffany. I
> wonder if lesbians communicate.)

Tiffany: Mr. Gary, where is the garbage can?
(I have already told them both, but do it
again.)

Joe: Mr. Gary, we had an incident last night, and
the betroom door got broke. (She wasn't
kidding. The door, which had been replaced
recently, was now in pieces.)

They explained to me that somehow the door got locked from
the inside, and they had to bust it down to get in. Now I realized
from past experience that lesbians liked to fight, but I just didn't see
it coming this early in our relationship. I replaced the door with a
nonlocking handset. The next call was actually why I was even writing about these two idiot lovers.

Tiffany said, "Mr. Gary, dit yo get a new mailbox key fo us yet?"

I replied, "Yes, Tiffany, I actually gave it to Joe right in front of
you."

"Oh yeah, guess I forgot."

"It was then I told you both that the charge for the door was
$100, and the key was $10."

"No problem. You wants me to pay that with the rent or take it
off our deposit?"

"Our deal was, if you remember, that you would pay it with the
rent. By the way, when will I see you? It is the fourth of the month,
and late charges kick in on the seventh."

Tiffany did not respond.

"Hello, Tiffany?"

Tiffany replied, "What's yo talkin' 'bout? I paid yo the prorated
rents good through March."

"No, you paid for one half of February because you moved in
on the fifteenth. March rent is due on the first, and it is now the
fourth. We went over this when you moved in."

"But I thought we were good to the end of March before we
owed you."

"No, March rent is now due, and the late charge goes into effect on the seventh. If I don't receive the rent by the tenth, I must give you an eviction notice."

"I'm confused. You mean I gots to pay you up front fo something I hasn't used yet?"

"Yes, I gets da money up fronts, and I lets you stay out da month."

"That's crazy. Who ever heard of paying fo something you hasn't used yet? When I goes to the restaurant, I eats my food before I pays fo it."

"Have you ever rented before?"

"Yeah."

"When was the rent due?"

Tiffany did not respond.

"Hello?"

"Well, if I was in bidness, I wouldn't have da rents due on the first."

"Den you wouldn't be in bidness very long."

This call went on and on for over an hour before she finally hung up on me. I was so mad and frustrated at the end of this call that I kicked the dog and picked a fight with my wife. Thirty minutes later, Tiffany called and said she would have the money to me on Thursday. (I chalked up this call as an Ebonics lesson.)

The most common calls I receive are from the good old country folk of Arkansas. The low-end housing we offer is right in line with the hardworking minimum wage earners of this state. Most are looking for a clean, safe, and affordable place to live for a spell. Phone conversations are a fairly good way to weed out the thorns and pick the cream of the crop. The following are examples of calls I have received over the years.

> Caller: Y'all got some trailers to rent? (When
> reading this, think deeeeeep South.)
> Me: Yes, we offer a nice selection of one-, two-,
> and three-bedroom mobile homes to lease.

Caller: Not *too* nice I hope. I ain't got much money.

Me: Well, our one-bedrooms go for $400 and a $200 deposit. Our two-bedrooms go for $500 and a $300 deposit. Our three-bedroom homes go for $600 with a $400 deposit. How much can you afford, and what size will you need?

Caller: Probably the cheapest you got, but can I work out the deposit?

Me: If you want a one-bedroom, what I need from you up front is $400 for rent plus $200 deposit, and the utilities must be in your name before I hand over the keys.

Caller: You mean, I have to pay all the utilities, and you won't let me work off the deposit?

Me: That is correct. Do you have any pets?

Caller: Um… *Click.*

On to the next call…

Caller: Tell me about these trailers you got to rent.

Me: Well, sir, how many bedrooms do you need?

Caller: Probably just one. My sister is kicking me out of her house, so I need it today. (I never like urgency.) I can get a ride over there, but I won't have any money until I find a job. Are you hiring?

Me: So let me just recap. You are homeless, with no job, no money, and no car, right?

Caller: Yeah.

Me: *Click.*

A good portion of calls I get are from single mothers. Lord knows I do all I can for these women. Many of them are out on their own trying to raise multiple children with little or no help from baby daddy. The call from Jennifer, a single mother with two small children, stands out above all the others. Our first conversation went like this.

> Jennifer: I'm looking for a two-bedroom for my kids and me.
> Me: I have a two-bedroom for $400 and—
> Jennifer: I'll take it. (A bit urgent, but I went further with her.)
> Me: Slow down a little and let me ask a few questions.
> Jennifer: All right.
> Me: Are you working? Do you have a car? What is your urgency?
> Jennifer: Yes, I work. Yes, I have a car, and I am going through a horrible divorce.
> Me: (Something made me ask a question that I have never asked before and hope to never ask again.) Will he be a problem for you?
> Jennifer: Only if he finds me. (Five of the scariest words ever spoken.)

Wanting to help this desperate young mother, I rented her unit number 21. She stayed for a very short time, and the rest is horrible history. (It's in chapter 15.) He found her (allegedly).

On a much lighter note, occasionally I will get a phone request for a *space* to rent. Now our park has been at full capacity with no vacant spaces available for at least ten years. If and when I get a call for a space and if it's a slow day, I will entertain the caller with information while being as cordial and polite as possible. (Actually, I do it for my own entertainment.) One such call went like this.

> Caller: You got any spaces available?
> Me: What size mobile home do you have, sir?

> Caller: It ain't for a trailer. It's for my log home.
> My SOB landlord is kicking me off his
> motherf—— property, and I need to move
> it fast.
> Me: Sir, we are a mobile home park and don't
> have a space for a log home.
> Caller: Well, then F—— YOU!

Minutes later, my caller ID showed an incoming call from the same number.

> Caller: I'm so sorry. I borrowed my phone to a
> friend, and I didn't know he was gonna go
> crazy on you like he did. I am so sorry.
> Me: Please tell your friend he needs to relax and
> check his attitude. I understand he is in a
> trying position, but I was only attempting
> to lend my assistance.

The next morning, I got a call from the same number.

> Caller: You got any spaces available?
> Me: Sir, I believe that we spoke yesterday, and
> you told me to *f—— myself*.
> Caller: Oh yeah. Sorry about that… *Click*.

I wonder if the jerk ever found a place for his log home. But like my wife says, by not having a space for this guy, "We dodged yet another bullet." We are getting good at bullet dodging.

One crazy call I got was from a lady who had a friend in dire need of a place to live. The story told to me immediately sounded familiar and went as follows.

> Caller: A friend of mine needs a place to rent
> ASAP. (Sense urgency, get more info.)
> Me: What is her urgency?

Caller: Her mother just died and her a-hole landlord is kicking her out. (This was now sounding *very* familiar.)

Me: Tell me more about her situation.

Caller: She is just having a hard time. A year ago, her husband tried to kill himself. Her daughter got pregnant, and the baby daddy was sent to prison for raping another woman.

Me: What is your friend's name?

Caller: Laura Potlicker. (I already knew, but I was messing with the friend.)

Me: So Laura is alone now. Does she work?

Caller: She works at Ho-Jo and has a fiancé who beats her. She's trying to shake him.

Me: Please tell Laura that Gary says hi. (I had had enough fun, and besides, I was in the middle of a plumbing problem.)

Caller: What?

Me: My name is Gary, and I am the a-hole land-lord who is kicking her out. Also, have Laura thank the payroll manager at Ho-Jo. I have been receiving the checks from Laura's garnished wages.

Caller: *Click.*

It was Johnny Cochran, the famous defense attorney for O. J. Simpson, who said, "It's not possible to tell the color of a person's skin by talking to them on the phone." I beg to differ. When Ebonics is spoken to me, I think I'm safe to say the caller is black. But like Jerry Seinfeld says, "Not that there's anything wrong with that." As a matter of fact, I'm about as well versed in the language of Ebonics as I am in Spanglish or Southern. The only time I get to practice this strange way of speaking is when I get a call from someone "axing fo sum infumation on a three-betroom trailer fo rent." After sharing the next call I received, you tell me if Johnny is right.

Caller: Yo gots any tree-betroom troilers fo rents?
Me: Yeah, I gots me a real nice three-betroom fo rents.
Caller: How much do it be costen?
Me: It be costing $600 wit a $400 deposit. Let me axe yo how many chillins yo got wit chew?
Caller: I gots me bout tree kids. (She had seven.)
Me: Do baby daddy stay wit yo?
Caller: Which one?
Me: Never mind. Do yo gots chew a job?
Caller: Me an' my kids gets us govermint checks.

Anyway, the conversation went on like this. What chew think, do Johnny be right?

Not all the calls I receive are from people *looking* for rentals or spaces. When you have thirty-six units in a trailer park, many calls come from *existing* tenants who have a perceived need. The following is a smattering of calls I've fielded over the years.

- "Gary, come quick. My toilet is overflowing." (I have received this one many times.)
- "I smell gas in the house."
- "I don't want to bother you but my house is full of smoke."
- "There is a guy dressed in camo, walking around the park with an automatic rifle." (I located this nut and had him arrested. He said we were overrun with squirrels and he was just helping us out by killing them.)
- "Gary, come quick. There is a deer in my yard." (We live in the country, and this woman is a heavy drinker. I told her it would soon leave.)
- "My house smells like skunk." (It did!)

- "There is a snake in my yard." (Again, we live in the country.)
- "My neighbors are fighting again." (They were.)
- A caller at 2:00 a.m., of course, "I hear a baby crying outside my trailer." (I couldn't find it.)
- A caller at 2:30 a.m., "I found a baby walking around the park." (Parents were stone drunk.)
- "Can you come bail me out of jail?" (I did—it was her third DUI.)
- "Can you take me to get my car out of impound?" (This was related to the last call.)
- "Can you take me to rehab?" (This was *not* related to the last two calls.)
- "Gary-man, I was just gonna axe you if I could maybe wash yo car and truck fo some spare coin. My babies (they have four) need diapers and we surely would appreciates us a little help." (I get this same call every month, and our vehicles are always very clean.)
- "There is a pack of dogs running around the park." (We live in the country.)
- "My car battery is dead." (I have received this many times; I have good jumper cables.)
- "My car is out of gas." (I have received this many times; I keep cans of gas on hand.)
- "We have no heat." (I have received this many times; I light the pilot.)
- "We have no hot water." (I have received this many times; I light the pilot.)
- "We have no electric." (I have received this many times; I flip the breaker.)
- "We have no water." (I tell them to pay their bill.)
- "I lost my keys." (I have received this more than many times.)
- "I'm watching my next-door neighbor pee in his yard." (He admitted it to me.)

- "There is a frog in my toilet." (There was. I captured and freed him.)
- "My kids heard a snake in the kitchen." (Only certain, very dangerous snakes make noise. It was a cicada in the exhaust fan above the stove.)
- "I have a flat tire." (I have a compressor.)
- "My neighbor's music is too loud." (It was.)
- "Gary, I gots yo rents fo yo." (I tell them my home and office are easy to find.)

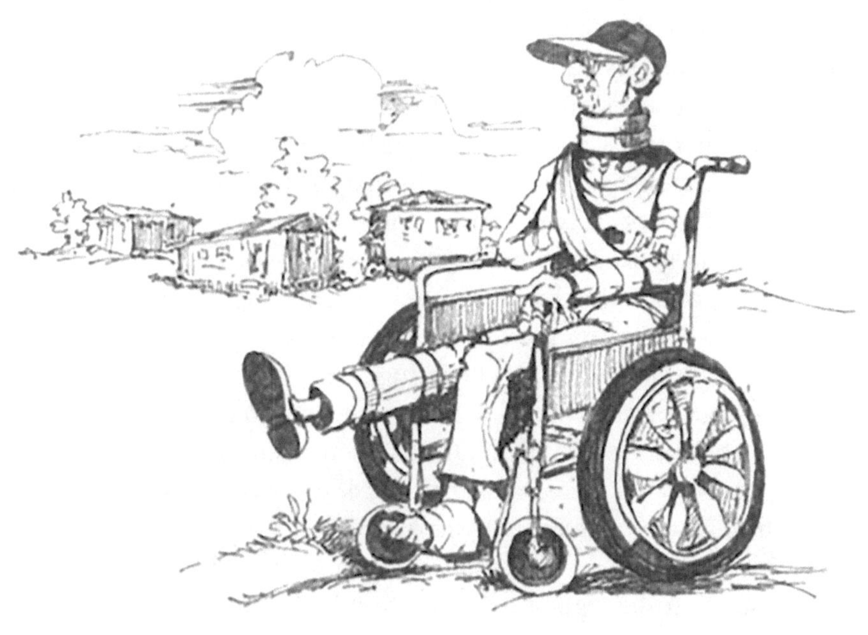

CHAPTER 9

Accidents, Injuries, Illnesses

Developing, managing, and maintaining a trailer park can be very hazardous to one's health. The following, in alphabetical order, are just some of the injuries and illnesses I have received over the years: abrasions, blood blisters, blunt trauma, breaks, bruises, bumps, burns, concussions, cracks, cuts, dislocations, heart attack, hernias, hyperextensions, prostate cancer (probably not related to mobile home park managing), pulls, punctures, ruptures, separations, slivers, sprains, stings, strains, tears, and tears.

Yard care is an important part of maintaining an attractive mobile home park. The nicer and neater the yards, the better the clientele will be interested in renting from you. The first trailer park we owned was two acres on the lake, and the homes were stacked on top of one another. All I needed was a push mower, a rake, and a Weed eater to maintain the lawns. The minimal yards were so small I could cut the entire park in two hours. One hour of weed eating and the park had that well-manicured look everyone loves.

One day, within thirty minutes of finishing the task of weed eating, I was trimming around a power pole, which had telephone and cable lines stapled to it. The string from the Weed eater snagged the lines, causing them to pull away from the pole. This caused the staples to become projectiles. One of them went shooting into my leg. Now my pants were stapled to my lower extremity by the two rusty, dirty, three-quarter-inch sharp points of the fastening implement. My first reaction was to jerk my pants away from my leg, causing the staple to be ripped from my flesh and leaving two puncture holes. The wound and eventual scars looked as though a snake or possibly a vampire had bitten me.

Another yard-care-related injury involved more creativity than the last. After a particularly windy storm, many branches of the trees in the park were left broken and hanging. Donning my tree trimmer's hat, I gathered the tools to remedy the damage done by the storm. A twenty-foot extension ladder and a chain saw were my weapons of choice. Starting the saw on the ground (it's hard to start a chain saw while standing on a ladder), I climbed toward the first sad broken limb. It was then I realized the branch was a bit higher than the ladder could reach.

Ignoring the warning, *"This rung should not be used as a step,"* I used it anyway. Standing on the top rung of the ladder, bear-hugging the tree with my left arm, and reaching the saw toward the broken limb with my right hand, I felt movement of my perch. The ladder fell from under my feet, causing the arm holding the saw to flail wildly. In doing so, the blades of the rotating chain made contact with the quadriceps of my right leg, tearing into flesh and muscle. Hanging there for what seemed like hours and hoping nobody was watching this high-flying act, I dropped the saw and shimmied down the tree. Most of the rest of the day was spent in the emergency room, getting stitched back together. (Just another scar for chicks to dig!)

The 9N and 8N Ford tractors I own have done much of the work developing the mobile home park: blading, scraping, and leveling the earth to define roads and trailer pads with the 8N and bushhogging and clearing the—until now—untouched property with the 9N.

In the early years, money was very tight, so I could only afford one battery between the two tractors. I would switch the battery from one to the other as needed. One day, while making the switch, I disconnected the leads and picked the battery up and out from its mounting hole. While transporting it to the other tractor, it slipped from my hands, falling to the ground. When the battery hit the ground, the corrosive acid splashed straight up into my face and eyes. So it was back to the ER once again, this time to get an optical flush before I went blind.

The final yard-care-related injury that I will share involves insects. The second park, which we currently own, is sixteen acres, with the front eight developed into a mobile home park. The back eight had been relatively untamed, so it has required some degree of maintenance. Once or twice a year, I bushhog the long wild grass to a more manicured look. Using my ancient Ford 9N with its bush-hog attachment, I maneuver around the trees and stumps, cutting all the grass, weeds, and small saplings which had grown since the last cutting.

One time, within reach of the finish line, I plowed through an old rotten stump, causing the mower to stall. Immediately, I felt as if unknown assassins from all directions were shooting at me. In actuality, what had happened was I disturbed the hive of ground-dwelling yellow jacket bees. These insects are relentless in defending their home, which I had just destroyed.

Receiving dozens of stings from the angry bees, it was then I was introduced to anaphylactic shock. Although this incident was more an illness than injury, it did teach me to wear long sleeves and pants while bushhogging and to always carry an EpiPen in the event I should ever run into the venomous, stinging bastards again.

The remodeling, repairing, and maintaining of rentals present very good opportunities for injury. The repair of a wobbly toilet is easily fixed by a wedge or shim. I like to use a cedar shake shingle for its shape, and they are usually easy to customize for the job of stabilizing the toilet. While sitting on the unleveled toilet I was attempting to correct, I had the shingle on my leg, ready to score. I was using a box blade knife to cut a line halfway through so I could then break the shingle to the proper size. Apparently I used too much pressure on the cedar shake because while scoring, it broke with a snap, and my downward pressure of the knife continued directly into my thigh. Pulling the razor-sharp blade from my leg, I saw a gaping two-inch bloody gash.

The ER doctors are starting to call me by my first name; I also may have heard something about "an accident waiting to happen."

One year after an Achilles tendon repair and rehab from a racquetball injury, I decided it was time to do a complete remodel on a rental unit. This included taking out and replacing all the old windows. Loading all the nasty, broken, and nonfunctional windows on my flatbed trailer, I backed it to my illegal landfill on the back eight acres, where I dump all unwanted materials that wouldn't burn. After unloading most of the windows from the trailer, I pulled the rest to the tail end and stepped off to remove and toss them into the ravine. They say, "Watch out for that first step," and they are right. Stepping backward off the trailer, my foot inadvertently landed on one of the discarded windows, with the sound of glass breaking. A sick feeling overwhelmed me with the knowledge of what I had just done. The broken glass tore through the newly rehabbed tendon.

It was then off to the ER for more needle and thread.

Cool sealing or roof coating is a common task, which must be done on a regular basis in the maintenance of mobile homes. Manufacturers recommend that roofs be treated every five to seven years to ensure problems such as leaks don't occur.

After neglecting unit number 3 for more years than recommended, I decided it was time to spread some of the liquid rubber to its upper surface. Climbing atop the roof for initial inspection, I discovered it was well overdue for my attention. With the third step onto the roof, my right leg went crotch deep into the living room of number 3. I *slowly* extricated my leg from the hole so I wouldn't end up entirely inside the home. When my leg was fully out, I noticed a great amount of pain in my knee, and it was locked in an extended position. Limping down the ladder and all the way home, I immediately called my orthopedic surgeon (I have him on speed dial) and was operated on two days later. Arthroscopic surgery repaired my meniscus, and after three months of rehab, my knee was good as new.

The plumbing infrastructure of our first mobile home park was ancient and a constant headache with leaks, clogs, and breaks. The replacement of all water and sewer lines proved to be a huge but necessary undertaking. With the homes being situated so close together, all digging had to be done by hand. There was no room to use a trencher or backhoe. I found the digging between each trailer fairly easy and was able to enjoy the heat, sun, and humidity of the Arkansas summer. However, the digging and picking under the homes in the cramped dark and dampness proved to be less enjoyable.

The project took the better part of six months with head-banging, blister-busting, muscle-tearing, and sweat-soaked twelve-hour days. But in the end, we had brand-new, top-of-the-line, carefree water and sewer lines, which would last the life of the park. My body did not fare so well. With all the repetitive motion of picking, digging, and shoveling, I developed a severe case of what is known as tennis elbow. This called for another visit to my friendly orthopedic surgeon, and after repair to the tendon in my elbow, I was ready to dig again.

Back in the days when we catered to overnight travel trailers, December through March was prime time for the Snowbirds to descend upon us. This was when many Yankees would make the trip south for warmer climates. In preparation for their arrival, I would always make sure the travel trailer pads were clean and that water, sewer, and electric were in good working order.

One day, after hearing from a regular customer from the North that they would be arriving the next day, I set out to do my usual checklist of conditions of the spaces. After cleaning all the downed leaves and a few small branches, it was time to check out the utilities. I found the water line had full pressure and the sewer line was free and clear of any obstructions.

Then it was on to the electric service. One week previous, I had called the local electric company to have the service turned on. In order to assure it was indeed on, I had to get into the meter box and wire a plug into the system. I would then plug in a tester to check the voltage.

First pulling off the face of the meter box, I then began to loosen the wire connector bolts with a wrench. I must have touched both bolts with the wrench because the next thing I remember—after seeing a humongous flash—was lying on ground, flat on my back, ten feet from where I had been standing. My shoes were smoking, and the wrench, still in my hand, had two weld marks that weren't there before.

The only side effect of this incident was that I am no longer able to grow eyebrows. As of yet, I have been unable to find anyone who can explain this phenomenon. Who needs eyebrows anyway?

After the burning of unit number 21, which was caused by the stupidity of the two geriatric homosexuals mentioned in chapter 1, I had to get the space ready for another trailer. The mess left by the fire department was horrible. (I wish that they had let it burn more.) Donning my postfire, trailer-burning demo uniform, I gathered up what I guessed I would need for the job. This consisted of pry bars, sledgehammer, reciprocating saw, and cutting torch.

The burnt-out trailer carcass had been an eyesore for about a month. This was the amount of time the insurance company took to file my claim. (This was also way back when I carried insurance on all my rentals.) Anyway, I got the check from the company and began the chore of cleanup. It was very slow going because it was the middle of winter, and we had received some snow and ice.

Everything was covered in a thin coating of the frozen stuff. Climbing upon the air-conditioning unit to get a better swing at a burnt wall, I slipped and fell. Now I am an ex-gymnast and pretty much know how to fall and not get hurt. This time was different.

Landing on my rib cage smack on the corner of the AC unit, I knew damage had been done. By the time I was able to make it home, I was coughing up blood. X-rays from the ER indicated I had two broken ribs and a punctured lung.

The burnt-out trailer carcass remained an eyesore until spring.

Billie "Smokestack" Patton was a lover of cigarettes who couldn't keep up with the mortgage on her home. I was able to purchase her house, number 37, through the repo agency.

Upon entering the home and inspecting what I had just bought, I found every surface covered thick with nicotine. The walls appeared to be tan, but with some soap and water applied to them, we found they were actually off-white wallpaper with a flowery pattern. The ceilings had to be painted, and I was able to save the carpet after steam cleaning it three times. All the windows seemed to have some type of tinting, but again, they, too, proved to be coated with the exhaled, nasty nicotine of Ms. Billie.

But while finishing the cleaning of one window, I was attempting to close it when it slammed down hard, catching the forefinger of my right hand. I knew it was broken when I looked at it. The finger made a ninety-degree turn at the first joint.

When extending my finger now, I am able to point around corners.

Many of these stories have actually occurred during the writing of this book. I have looked at the situations that happened as fodder for a bestseller. One such event occurred during the writing of chapter 10, "Handymen." After a six-month layoff from putting to paper things that happened to us over the span of forty years, one particular event is still very fresh in my mind.

On Monday, November 18, 2013, after a fun-filled day of playing pickleball and raking up piles of falling leaves in the park, I decided to call it a day and turn in early. Around midnight, I awoke to a strange feeling of pressure in my left armpit. My arm began to feel very heavy, and I got the cold shivers. Thinking that I had overdone it with all the activities the previous day, I did my usual cure-all and jumped into the hot tub. After ten minutes of stretching in the liquid, bubbling heat, I began to feel better and marked it off as just a strained muscle.

The next day, I got up feeling great and went off to play a very competitive game of tennis with friends. Postmatch, I went home and raked more leaves. After all, when it is fall in Arkansas, you've got to get rid of them when they are dry. Putting in another normal day in the life of me, I went to bed early. At or around midnight the feeling of someone pushing their fist in my left armpit awakened me.

This time the pressure was greater and was accompanied by the cold sweats, pain in my back and chest, and feeling like my arm weighed a ton. This condition came and went about five times with the pain and pressure getting worse with each episode. I made my way to the back bedroom, where my wife was sleeping, woke her up, and described what I was experiencing. Once again, I looked for relief in the hot tub, and it did seem to help. After getting out and while drying off with a towel, the pain and pressure came back with a vengeance. That was it for my wife. She had seen enough, so she got me dressed, and it was on to the ER.

Within several hours of my arrival to the ER, I experienced many firsts for me. The first, first was the EKG. The second was the nitroglycerin tablets. By this time I was beginning to understand where these caregivers were going. The third first for me was the blood/heart enzyme test, which showed negative, but they promised to give me another test in a couple of hours. The second enzyme test showed to be positive, proof that I indeed did have a heart attack. WTF!

I am the healthiest person I know, so how could this be? It turns out genetics and family history can play cruel tricks on a person.

The next first was off to the OR for a cardiac cath. This is actually a fun procedure where the doctor inserts a tube into the femoral artery in the groin, and it is pushed all the way through the body till it makes its way to the heart. I was given a numbing shot in my groin and a slight jolt of happy juice. This permitted me to be present during most of the procedure. I watched the monitor as the tube injected dye into certain veins in my heart. When the doctor came to a roadblock, all I heard was, "Got it." The *it* was an hourglass-shaped figure in a vein, which was not supposed to be there. The doctor explained this as a 95 percent blockage, and it happened to be in a major vein.

A few minutes later, I was the proud owner of two new stents in my heart and the newest member to the club. No one could have ever imagined that I would have this happen to me. But I vowed to be the very best recovery patient and do all that my doctor told me.

What this experience has taught me is to watch your diet and exercise, which I was pretty good at. Also have your blood pressure and cholesterol checked regularly. The most important thing I learned is to choose your parents wisely.

The next two visits to the hospital were back-to-back. It all started with a trip to my GP to get a full physical. I was turning fifty and thought it might be a good idea to find out if I was going to make it another half century.

An appointment was made with my doctor, who is a little, bitty person with possibly the smallest hands in Arkansas. I actually chose her because my last doctor had the hands of Hoss Cartwright from the TV show *Bonanza*. Digital prostate exams with him were not fun. Anyway, I figured I would be receiving said exam, so before I left home for my appointment, I stuck a lick-and-stick temporary tattoo of a Confederate flag to my left butt cheek. It was my thought that Dr. Small Hands would get a kick out of it when she was back there. She did! But I'm getting ahead of myself.

So the physical was going along as I had expected. My weight was taken along with temperature, heart rate, ear exam, blood sample, and the usual grab, turn head, and cough—the works. During the prostate exam portion of my physical, I thought my doctor was spending an inordinate amount of time with her probing. When I asked her what she was doing back there, her reply was, "I feel something out of the ordinary." She was on to something because when the results of my blood test came back, the PSA number was 2.4. Off to a specialist I went, where, after a biopsy, it was confirmed to be *prostate cancer*.

I've got to say that the biopsy was the worst part of this horrible adventure. The doctor perforates the rectum wall with a long needle, inserting it into the prostate gland. The needle pulls a plug from the prostate, and the sample is sent to pathology. One sample is bad enough, but I had ten taken. It was a very uncomfortable and painful procedure. Results from pathology were that two of the five samples, from the left lobe of my prostate, were positive for cancer. Not good news…it felt like a death sentence.

After doing some research on the subject, we discovered that this type of cancer is very slow-moving and very survivable. The plan of attack we chose was a radical prostatectomy. Since the cancer was totally encapsulated in the gland, it could be removed. Good news!

We scheduled the surgery with a new, young urologist and had the procedure. (He was fresh out of med school, and this, I believe, was his first radical prostatectomy.)

When I was in recovery, a friend stopped in and gave me a buckeye nut for good luck———a Southern tradition. When my doctor came to check on me, he saw the nut on my tray and asked how I got it. I got the feeling he thought it was the gland that he removed. Real quick I told him that pathology had it freeze-dried and sent up to me as a souvenir. When he discovered I was lying, he said the nut looked surprisingly like the body part he removed from me.

Three days later, I was released from the hospital, but only after I cut the world's longest fart. I am not kidding; it was of Olympic quality. The bad thing was a lady friend had just come to my room with well-wishes. I bet she wished that she hadn't! My doctor told me he would not release me without this event occurring. Well, it did, and I had a witness.

My next trip to the hospital was *two* days later. I started to have terrible pain in my lower back on the left side. Back to the hospital we went. We were doing the ER evaluation when I was asked on what level the pain was on a 1–10 basis. At that time the pain was very high, so I said 9. I was being asked more questions when I threw up on the nurse's shoe. We determined the pain was then at a level 10, and I was experiencing a kidney stone.

The next day, lithotripsy (bombing the stone with a laser) was tried, to no avail. The stone was so hard that the laser just bounced off it. The only other remedy was to go in and get it. The same doctor who performed my prostatectomy came to help me again. He was not happy with the prospect of retrieving the stone from the same plumbing of mine, which had just been rerouted days previous. He did it anyway. Back to the OR we went.

When I came out of surgery—which was a success—the nurses were telling me how similar the male prostatectomy is to a female hysterectomy and a kidney stone is to giving birth. Leave it to me to have a hysterectomy, then give birth.

I have always been in touch with my female side, but these experiences brought me even closer.

CHAPTER 10

Handymen

When first taking over the business back in 1977, it was out of necessity that I did all the repairs, maintenance, and yard work. There was just no way I could afford to pay someone to do all that was needed to keep the mobile home park functioning. In the first year, it became clear to me I would have to become an expert in plumbing, electrical, carpentry, masonry, and yard care plus anything else that would come up and need fixing, including people.

After thirty-six years, I felt like I had earned master's degrees in all such fields, along with PhDs in psychology, sociology, and advanced first aid and emergency care. It had always been my dream to have a live-in handy person who rented from me and could handle all the problems that arose in the day-to-day functioning of the park. It was only after the sale of our first park that I felt we could afford to hire out work.

Then came Dave.

Dave and his brother Malvern spent their first six months with us, renting a small two-bedroom right across the driveway from our home. We didn't get to know them at all as Malvern stayed in their home and Dave was gone most days till after dark. We found out later that he was spending all his time at the bar down the street. Then one day they were gone.

About one year later, Dave and Malvern showed up again, needing a place to stay. They explained their situation to me, claiming they had no money but were interested in working off the rent. I agreed to let them stay in our crummiest one-bedroom and put them to work. Malvern was more than happy to rake leaves, pick up branches, and trim hedges.

Dave turned out to be quite talented in all types of repairs and was an excellent carpenter. He also had all his own tools, which was a big plus in my book. I began giving Dave lists of things that needed repair. As long as I was right there with him, Dave was able to complete the task. But I found that if I wasn't actually with him on the job, the necessary repairs didn't get done, and my tools, which ended up being used, did not get put away.

When I would go looking for Dave to ask why he didn't finish the job, I would inevitably find him down at the corner bar. It took me a while to finally figure out that Dave didn't like the small jobs that filled my days but still needed to be done. Tasks like water leaks, replacing light switches, fixing soft spots in floors, relighting heaters, changing out water heaters that had gone bad, fixing a leak in a roof, replacing glass in a broken window, and painting a bathroom—all fell into the category of not being big enough for Dave.

So when I decided to renovate an old house on the property, Dave volunteered his services. This actually turned out to be a much larger job than I thought. We were going to add a twenty-foot-by-twenty-foot section to enlarge a bedroom and the kitchen, move some walls around to change up the living space, put in a new bathroom, and replace the entire roof with steel. Dave and I were both excited about the project, and we dove into it. Each day we would put in about six to eight hours; then I would walk home. Dave, however, would stay at the house, sit on a bucket, drink beer, and think about what was to be done the next day.

Each morning, I would show up at the jobsite and find twenty-four beer cans scattered about the yard. Dave would be there, ready to start after he told me about all the changes he had come up with, most of which were pretty good ideas and in the end made the house a much better place. The work lasted four to five weeks with Dave and me side by side in harmony.

That's about the time I went out of town on one of my getaways. Dave promised to continue the work on the house, and his bro, Malvern, would help. When I got back one week later, I found that virtually no work had gone on, and there was twice the number of beer cans scattered about than should have been. When I confronted Dave about this, his reply was he had come up with many more changes to the project and was waiting for my approval. Dave had been drinking and thinking instead of working. This is, of course, what he is best at.

After I was back home, we got back on track and finished the remodel, which turned out fantastic.

After the big renovation of the home, I did ask Dave and another tenant, Todd, to do one last job for me. A small deck with stairs off the back door of a rental was needed. I bought the materials, and Dave and Todd set off to complete the task. I checked on his progress around noon and was disappointed that the work wasn't further along. But they said the job would be done by the end of the day.

At 4:00 p.m. I came back to check on the deck. What I found was Dave and Todd both passed out on the ground, which was littered with beer cans. The work they had done looked like something a five-year-old would do. That was it for me. After waking them out of their drunken stupor, I screamed at them for twenty minutes. I specifically told Dave that I was done with him as a handyman, and if he didn't get help for his problem, I was done with him as a tenant as well.

That night I drove them both to AA. Todd did okay. After that day, Dave attended AA meetings on a regular basis until he fell hard off the wagon (actually it was a scooter, which I had bought for him) drunker than Cooter Brown.

Sometime between 2:00 and 4:00 a.m. that morning (when else?), Dave called me from the hospital, obviously still hammered, asking me to pick him up. I was already up (I get up early), to get ready to go to a tennis tournament; I told him I could get him in a couple of hours.

Ten minutes later, I got a call from an Arkansas state trooper asking when I would be there. I said it would take at least two hours and asked why Dave wasn't in jail. The trooper said he would be taken there now for lying to him. It seemed Dave had told the trooper that I would be coming to the hospital immediately to drive him home. I told the trooper to throw away the key to Dave's cell.

Dave was released from the drunk tank after twelve hours and walked home. When I saw him the next day, he had a broken shoulder, and his face looked like a pizza. I took Dave to a rehab facility, where he remained for three months.

To this day I believe that Dave has not had a drink. But he still owes me for the scooter. He continues to live with his brother in a trashy old house in a bad part of town, and he still doesn't have a job. In a way I miss the old Dave. He was the most talented handyman and happiest drunk I had ever met.

The biggest benefit I lost when Dave quit drinking and moved on was the enormous number of aluminum cans I would no longer collect and recycle for cash.

The aforementioned Todd from the last story, who I had taken to the AA meeting, became my next on-site handyman. He had no driver's license, no car, and no job. And he had wants and warrants out of Michigan for child support, so…of course… I gave him a shot.

Unlike my previous helper, Todd was ready, willing, and able to do anything I asked him. He turned out surprisingly capable of doing all jobs—big or small—in the park. A bonus with Todd was that I didn't have to watch over his shoulder every minute of the day for him to get the work done. He was also the best Weed eater guy I ever had. When he broke the Weed eater, he could fix it. And when he broke the chain saw, he could fix it.

The problem was the three boys Todd had adopted. These three kids were tornados, tearing up everything in sight. Breaking water lines, stuffing sewer lines with dirt and rocks, and breaking windows were all part of their MO. Todd was always apologetic and fixed the damage, saying, "Boys will be boys." These eight- to eleven-year-old kids were like none I had ever seen. They were horrible and made me want to turn the park into strictly adult.

In one week's time, his middle kid stole cigarettes from a tenant and smoked them all in ten minutes. A few days later, the same kid was playing chicken with cars on the highway until one of the cars turned out to be driven by a cop. A few days after this incident, I caught Todd's oldest throwing a knife at another kid, whom he had tied to a tree.

This was my breaking point. I really didn't want to lose Todd, but how could I tell him to get rid of his three terrorists? I permitted the Todd tribe to stay till school let out for summer, then I kicked them out. Before they left, I had a long conversation with my ex-handyman about his parenting skills, and as of this writing, it remains to be seen what, if anything, will be done.

I can't wait to see what these kids will get into as teenagers!

Another tenant I hired on as yard guy was Martin Black. Marty was a fireman for the city and needed to supplement his income, as most firemen do. Apparently they aren't paid much. Anyway, Marty worked the Weed eater for me for two years and did a fantastic job. The great thing about Martin was that he was immune from the oil of the poison ivy plant, unlike me, who, if I even looked at the plant, would be suffering for three to four weeks with an itchy red rash. Marty single-handedly eradicated 50 percent of the horrible plant from the property, for which I am eternally thankful.

However, toward the end of his second season of working for me, I began to get calls from area neighbors. It seems that when they were driving by the park and Marty was trimming along the road, they were assaulted with cussing, yelling, and screaming. Several even had rocks thrown at their vehicles. When I asked Marty about the matter, he said he didn't remember anything like this happening.

I immediately suspected that my yard guy had a bad problem with alcohol. The Weed eater was confiscated, and he moved out shortly after.

Years later, my belief was confirmed when I ran into Marty at the only AA meeting I ever attended (the one with Dave and Todd).

It is possible and advantageous to develop a relationship with a handyman if one intends to employ that person multiple times. One such person was Jim Bell, my exterminator, who I have already mentioned in my previous chapter on pests.

Dr. Bugg, as we call him, had been keeping the pests at bay in our parks for thirty-six years. After seeing someone every three months for 3 1/2 decades, you get to know them pretty well and, in our case, become good friends.

On a quarterly basis, Jim would give me a call saying it was time to hit the bugs. We would agree on a time, usually a Friday at 9:00 a.m., and he would show up and commence with the application of his insect-eradicating spray.

Without exception, Jim always had a joke or story to go along with the spraying of the first unit of the day. These jokes were usually leaning toward off-color, and I always made sure my wife was out of earshot since our home was first on the list to be done. Most of these jokes were third and fourth generation, which he recycled to me. But I never let Jim know it wasn't the first time he was sharing the dirty little tale with me. After all, he enjoyed the telling, and I enjoyed hearing the way he told each and every bad joke, no matter how many times I heard it.

Dr. Bugg's knowledge of crawling creatures was very extensive. He could see a bug—usually a roach—and tell me what kind it was, its breeding habits, and its expected lifespan. Also adding it could live off one drop of piss for six months. The only insect Jim wasn't equipped to eradicate with the poison mixture was spiders. He said the best way to eliminate spiders was with a broom or the heel of a shoe. I witnessed his shoe technique on many occasions, with much success. His kill rate was 100 percent—one squash of the heel, one dead spider.

After finishing up with the spraying of our home and office and hearing the dirty story for the umpteenth time, it was off to do the rounds of my rentals. Most of the time, I would notify the tenants a few days in advance that the exterminator would be coming and that they should have their homes in order for our visit. On these visits, I would also change heat and air filters and check for leaks and for soft spots in floors. Even with the advanced notice, many a home was found to be in an unkempt condition. Dirty dishes on tables, countertops, and in the sink…with garbage and dirty clothes knee-deep throughout the house. This always brought a colorful comment from my bug guy.

In the homes of my unemployed renters, Jim and I would find them sound asleep in bed or on the couch at 9:00, 10:00, 11:00 a.m. Being a firm believer in a positive work ethic, Dr. Bugg had no sympathy for these slimes of society. Many a time I witnessed Jim spraying 360 degrees around a groggy, worthless, nonworking slug. Then still within hearing distance, he would describe to me how he felt about the slimeball or slime bet.

There were a few tenants for whom Jim had a particular distain. Top on his list were Rick and Jackie in unit number 5. In Jim's eyes, this pair was of no apparent good for humanity. Since both were fat, lazy, nonworking, unfriendly complainers, Jim was always happy to skip number 5 when they didn't answer the door after his ever-so-light tapping.

One particular visit, which stands out in my mind, occurred after the male half of the couple had been on a rigorous diet and exercise program. Seeing Rick in his new slim body prompted Dr. Bugg to remark how good he looked. This brought on the comment from Jackie that "nobody ever says anything good about me."

So Jim, who is not afraid to say what he thinks, said to her, "Well, you *are* still fat and ugly." I just love this guy.

Many times Jim, whose real name is Tom, witnessed me yelling and screaming at a renter for nonpayment of rent or living like a slob. He always had my back and supported my rantings at any individual blight on society.

At the time of this writing, Jim, after forty years of working with toxic chemicals, has succumbed to full-blown cancer throughout his body. He is currently doing radiation therapy, which has caused him to miss our last couple of appointments.

The last couple of phone conversations we had were not good. It sounds like he is giving up and just wants it all to be over. If he goes, he will be very much missed, not only for his bug-killing expertise but also for his friendship.

There are times when I just can't do the necessary repairs due to time constraints. That is when I have to refer to my list of experts. Those on my list have proven to be reliable, trustworthy, and competent.

The day before leaving for one of my adventures, I rented a unit in which the gas company—for the previous renter's nonpayment—had turned off the gas, unbeknown to me. It turns out that when the gas has been off for more than two months, all the pipes in the house to the meter must be pressure-tested by a licensed plumber. This is an easy job, which I have done many times in the past. But since I was leaving the next day, I called Steve from Econo-Rooter. I had used Steve for a few jobs in the past, which he had completed with success. He said he would be out the next day to do the work, and I told him I would leave a signed blank check in the drop box.

I departed early the next morning thinking all was good. Around noon that day, I got a call from my new renter saying the plumber hadn't shown up. I gave him Steve's number and told him to call to find out what was causing the delay. After several calls, my renter was able to connect with Steve and was told the job would be done by 5:00 p.m. It wasn't.

The next day, my renter tried to raise Steve with no success. Around noon, he gave up on my plumber and tried the yellow pages to locate another plumber to do the work. Starting at the top of the list of plumbers was Any Time Plumbing. Placing a call to them and explaining the situation, my renter learned that Steve had also called Any Time Plumbing to get them to do the work the day before.

Mike from Any Time described to my renter what a slimeball Steve actually was and that he, Mike, would be happy to pressure-test the lines for us. Upon further investigation, we found out that Steve was not a licensed plumber, had done shoddy work all over the county, and in fact had received a fine from the plumbing inspector for $5,000 for doing work he was not licensed to do.

Keep in mind that I was hiking slot canyons in Utah while this was all going on. It was two days later when I remembered the blank check for Econo-Rooter in the box back home. I called my father to snag the check from the box and tear it up. It was too late. When Dad got there, the check was gone. After giving him my account and check numbers, Dad called the bank only to find that the check had been cashed for the sum of $210. *Shit!* Not only had the SOB not done the work, but Steve also snuck over and stole my check, made it out for $210, and cashed it. Bastard! Needless to say, I was *pissed*.

I called Steve every day multiple times. On the first few calls, which were answered, he said he had made a horrible mistake and would make it right and get the money back to me. After that, he stopped answering my calls, so I left messages—tons of messages. None were acknowledged by Steve.

My dark side kicked in—developing scenarios in my mind, ways to get even with my ex-plumber. I did come up with many elaborate and creative plans to take revenge on the jerk. But in the end, I am a somewhat law-abiding business owner and didn't want to spend time in jail. So I pretty much wrote it off as a learning experience. I did notify the Better Business Bureau and lodged a complaint. Big deal, it seems that I was not the first.

But at least my buddy Steve knows that I know what an a-hole he is!

Fast Eddie was a short, heavyset, middle-aged man from Philadelphia. He came with a gorgeous, buxom blonde, who was half his age and claimed to be his wife. The couple rented number 23, which was right on the lake. These foreigners were a strange fit for the park, but we figured that we were equal-opportunity landlords, so we gave them a shot. Neither Eddie nor his girlfriend/wife had a vehicle or a job that we could see. They would hole up in the home with no apparent human contact. When the first of the month came, Fast Eddie always paid the rent in full by cash, which he would count off from a huge roll of bills.

In the fall, Eddie took an interest in yard work around the park, raking leaves and picking up sticks. The park never looked better, and I, being the yard boy for years, never had it so good. About this time Eddie told me that he had a cousin looking for a place to live. Unit number 24 next to his came open, so we signed Phil from Philly to a six-month lease. As with Eddie, Phil came with no car and no job, which we saw as strange. But like Eddie, Phil paid in cash on the first of the month and stayed to himself.

When summer arrived, Eddie and his lady friend's child showed up. Until now the park had always been strictly adult, so one can only imagine the stir this brought to our little community. It really got bad when the little darling tried to learn to ride a bike for the first time. Fifty percent of the tenants' parked cars got scratched or dinged. Complaints were made, a scolding was handed out, and amends were taken care of. Eddie paid off each damaged tenant from the same roll of bills in his pocket, which never seemed to change in size.

One day in late summer, Phil from Philly went AWOL. When asked about his cousin, Eddie said that he probably went home. We thought nothing of it and went about our business.

Then one day in the fall, while Eddie was raking leaves around his house, three federal marshals came out of nowhere from three different directions. With only the lake as his choice for escape, Eddie did what any felon would do while trying to evade capture. He dove in, only then remembering that he couldn't swim. Standing in waist-deep water, the marshals coaxed Fast Eddie back to shore. Placing him in cuffs and into the back of a government car, that was the last time I saw my yard guy.

I truly liked Eddie, and he made my life, for a time, much easier. Over the next few days, Eddie's lady friend told me how much he liked me. And he wanted me to know that he really enjoyed his short stay with us. She also stated that Eddie would die in prison.

About one month later, I received a collect call from Eddie saying that he couldn't say much. But he wanted me to know that "I didn't kill nobody." I really miss Fast Eddie.

CHAPTER 11

This Chapter Is Garbage

The disposal of garbage for a fairly large mobile home park can be a daunting undertaking. Let's face it, everyone generates trash each and every day, some a great deal more than others. The problem is what to do with it.

Years ago when I developed our second park, there was a trash transfer station about three miles down the road. Twice a week, I would collect the rubbish from each tenant, toss it into the bed of my

101

old pickup truck, and deliver it all to the station. This wasn't so bad when we only had ten units in the park. When I developed and filled ten more spaces, my truck suddenly became too small. It's amazing how much trash can be produced by twenty families. We hung in there, hauling the garbage using my old truck and a sixteen-foot flat-bed trailer for many years.

One benefit of hauling everyone's trash was I got first shot at all the good stuff that was thrown out. The first thing I did when I got to the transfer station was to go through all the bags and separate the aluminum cans. (I made a lot of money cashing in cans.) This gave me the idea, years later, to have everybody in the park recycle.

Going through all the individual bags also helped me to keep an eye on people who I thought might be a problem. If I came across a bag with drug paraphernalia (hypodermic needles, small bags with a white powdery substance, traces of a leafy green material, or any other suspicious items), I would then have a talk with the alleged offender. The way I knew who to talk to was easy. If I found a drug item, I would then dig further in the bag in hopes of finding a piece of mail or discarded prescription bottle with the name of the tenant on it. (They just don't teach this stuff in mobile home park management school.)

Besides the aluminum cans and drug stuff, I would be on the lookout for anything of value. When I discovered pots, pans, old clothes, bedding, towels, and unopened cans of food—all from the same unit—I not only knew I could find a family in need of the stuff, but it also told me that someone was moving out without notice. Then I would go have a talk with them. (I should open the Gary Strakshus School of Mobile Home Park Management.)

Eventually the county came to the rescue and implemented a door-to-door trash pickup service. My prayers had been answered.

So for several years, my job was garbage-free, with the county picking up and disposing the tons of trash that my people kept producing. I must admit that I did miss all the good junk and aluminum cans, but I filled my new downtime with developing more spaces for mobile homes. When I was done, we had thirty-eight rental spaces, of which we owned thirty. Each unit was charged individually by the county for waste management.

After three years of this system, the county discovered they had a problem. It seemed that many renting tenants would ignore the bill sent to them by the county for services rendered, racking up thousands of dollars of unpaid bills. It wasn't only my tenants who were neglecting the county, but thousands of other renters from all over the area were also doing the same. I was surprised at the list of names and amounts from renters in my park who were negligent. We have always prided ourselves in choosing good, responsible, and honest people to live in our community. So I went around with the list that the county furnished and asked (demanded) each offender to man up and pay their fair share. Those who decided to pay for the past and future services were allowed to remain in the park. A few decided to slither away and wallow in their guilt.

The county then came up with a new billing system where the property owner would be responsible for all trash pickup. Fine with me! I just bumped everyone's rent the amount they had been paying the county and paid the county's bill when I got it. The county got 100 percent payment for their service, and all my tenants were paying their fair share.

Then I decided to total up what Garland County was bringing in each year from garbage collection from our little thirty-eight-unit park. It was flabbergasting to me to see the amount we were paying. Between $4,000 and $6,000 each year seemed a bit steep just for loading, hauling, and dumping our trash into a hole. Keep in mind that I used to do this job for free when we had the transfer station down the road.

It seemed to me that this could be done more efficiently and at less cost, so that was when I looked into having one large green bin for the entire park. This—it turns out—was *brilliant*! The bin was large enough to hold all the household garbage from the park for one week. The price was less than half of what we were paying for individual unit pickup. On top of that, I once again got first shot at all the good stuff by climbing in and digging through the big green dumpster.

At this same time, we implemented a mandatory recycling program for all tenants. I built a covered recycling station next to the green bin. Baskets were furnished for aluminum cans, plastics number 1 and number 2, newspaper, corrugated cardboard, and phone books. It wasn't long before most of my tenants were actually doing as I asked and separating most of their recyclables. Once a week, I would load up all the plastics, paper, and cardboard and transport it to a recycling station in the city. For this I didn't receive any money for my efforts, but it was (and is) the right thing to do for the environment. Every two weeks, I would load the aluminum cans in my truck and sell them to a scrap metal business in downtown Hot Springs. Receiving $30 to $40 every two weeks for the sale of aluminum has added up to a good amount and has been used to cater our annual trailer-park witch-burn bonfire each Halloween season.

Since the subject of the bonfire has come up, and it does have something to do with waste disposal, I must elaborate. The bonfire is an annual trailer park tradition, which has been a perk of the park for over thirty years. All year long we collect the dead, dying, or storm-damaged trees from the sixteen acres of property, cut them up, and heap the debris into one great pile. Included in the mound could be unused found lumber from a remodel project, old or damaged wood furniture, trashed doors from the feuding lesbian couple, and the occasional dead stray cat. Keep in mind that the bulk of the heap consisted of yard waste. Sometimes, a neighbor or friend would ask if they could add to our pile with their rotten fencing, an old picnic table, boxes and boxes of their books they didn't sell, or just some unwanted brush they cut from their yard. I have always been very accommodating, telling them to bring their contributions, but if they did, I told them they were obligated to also attend the annual bonfire.

Each contributor was also instructed to prepare and bring a potluck to share. Of course, they already knew this and used their contribution as an invitation to attend the biggest and most popular event of the year. The food has always been a fantastic and eclectic blend of creative dishes. And of course, I would arrange my favorite local BBQ restauranteur to cater the event, using the proceeds from recycled aluminum cans. In our early years, during the mideight-ies, people we didn't even know would show up to the burn in full Halloween costume.

The next morning after the party, I would walk down to the hot pile of smoldering embers only to find drunk and hungover partyers, guys dressed as Playboy Bunnies, girls as *hot* nurses, and a Little Red Riding Hood. It seemed that everyone had a good time.

In later years, when the mountains of yard waste were larger, I would invite the volunteer fire department to attend. The guys would show up with a pumper truck and little fireman hats for the kids of the park. They would make sure the fire didn't get out of con-trol and hand out hats to the children. They could also be found with heaping plates of food and perhaps an adult beverage. The assistant chief, who was also a resident of the park, told me that members of his group fought over the detail of attending our annual event.

Another tradition of our bonfire was a hayride for the kids. But on each run around the park, I would see many adults enjoying themselves in the straw-covered flatbed trailer.

After the cleanup and conclusion of each of our gatherings, Gay and I would slip into our hot tub with some Baileys and try to count all the people who attended. We determined that we enter-tained between sixty and eighty tenants, friends, mountain bikers, triathletes, churchgoers, neighbors, tennis players, pickleball players, firemen and women, handymen, and many folks we didn't know. Everyone always had a great time with many commenting that they couldn't wait for the next Halloween celebration. Early the next morning, we would go through all the garbage cans from the gather-ing and pull out all the aluminum cans in preparation for the fund-ing of the *next* bonfire.

Over the years, there have been more than a few renters who decided they didn't want to haul their trash up the hill to the dump-ster. I would discover this fact after the noncompliant jerks would move on. We have always furnished ten-foot-by-ten-foot storage buildings for all the thirty units that we own. Many times, after the tenant has left, we have found these storage units slam full with six months' worth of the nastiest garbage to be found.

One could imagine that summertime is the worst. After loading my truck with the vulgar crap, I then drive it up to the dumpster and begin the horrible task of going through each bag, separating all the recyclables. Did I mention that summer is the worst? That is when the smell and the maggots are at their maximum. One time I actually caught an offender with a shed full of his garbage before he skipped out on us. I made him help with the separation of recyclables. He toughed it out for the entire process, going through each bag, choking and gagging the whole time. This was an experience he will not soon forget and will never want to duplicate. I, on the other hand, was the benefactor of six months of aluminum cans from all his beer drinking.

The Crenshaw family was a young couple who joined our small community shortly after we began the development of the park. They arrived with one infant son and the smallest double-wide mobile home I had ever seen. We set them up in space number 1, and soon they had the home underpinned and a deck built off the front door. Tom Crenshaw had had an early-model red Firebird sports car since he was in high school, and I told him he could store it up the hill near the dumpster. This thing was a real POS with four flat tires, windows broken out, and totally filthy. The interior was even worse: dogs, cats, mice, and rats had been making this American classic their home for years before it got to its new resting spot on our property.

Years passed with not much contact between me and the Crenshaws. They seemed to go about their lives, staying to themselves in an almost invisible, unusual manner. Daphne Crenshaw had produced two more boys, and with the oldest now in his teens, we started to get complaints of the boys doing what highly active boys do. When a report came to me of their neighbors' windows being shot out along with those of passing vehicles, it was time for the cop of the park to jump into action. Bringing the bad news to the parents, I was assured the problem would be taken care of.

Shortly after this incident, a very large open-topped dumpster showed up in the front yard of space number 1. When I asked them what was going on, they told me they were cleaning out their home of unwanted junk and were buying a house. I told them this was great and that I always like seeing my people go after the American Dream. Amazingly, the huge dumpster was full to overflowing in a matter of days. After the trash receptacle was hauled to the landfill by the county, I asked Daphne where all the crap came from. She said that this pile was nothing and "I could fill three more bins just like that one." Of course, I took this as an exaggeration and didn't think of it again.

A couple months later, they closed on their new abode, and shortly after that, they moved out of space number 1. Several times I contacted them as to what the plans were for their now old double-wide. I showed an interest in purchasing the home and adding it to my stable of rentals. But I couldn't get an answer from them on how much they expected to get for the home. Months went by, and I continued to receive the lot rent payments from the Crenshaws through direct deposit (I wish all the units were empty, and I still got the rent).

More time went by. Then I received a call from a concerned tenant about the back door on unit number 1 being open. I immediately went down to investigate. Indeed the door was wide open and falling off its hinges. I didn't believe it was a break-in, but the thing was in rough shape from all the abuse it had seen from the Crenshaws' three boys. Being the inquisitive detective I am, I decided to see if there were any squatters located in the trailer. There weren't. What there was, however, was the worst case of hoarding I have ever had the "privilege" to observe. The *Hoarders* shows on TV had nothing on this one.

Cautiously stepping into the mud, and I mean *mud*room, I was instantly met with a pile of rubbish. Making my way into the kitchen, it got worse. The narrow path through the kitchen was lined on each side with junk and trash. Doors of cabinets were either hanging by one bent hinge or nonexistent. The faucet to the sink looked like it had been hit with a sledgehammer, and there were holes in the walls.

But the living room is where I found the mother lode. Not only was there broken furniture but also bags of clothes, many toys, yard tools, and seasonal decorations. These included multiple fake Christmas trees still with ornaments, strings of lights and tinsel,

Easter bunny blow-up figures, Thanksgiving turkey cutouts on the walls with big pink hearts, and ground hogs next to the turkeys. The Crenshaws seemed like a very celebratory family. But it was now the month of June with no holiday to celebrate.

Then I saw the crumpled-up, aboveground swimming pool on top of a pile in a corner… It made sense to me that summertime can be celebrated by a nice cool dip. Onward I went toward what I believed to be the dining area. With the amount of head-high garbage in this room, I can guarantee there had been no family sit-down dinners in recent times. Squeezing my way down the walkway to the master suite (which can better be described as a master mess), I found half-full boxes and bags—shoulder-high—covering the room with, I think, a bed under it all.

In the master bath, I found evidence that the Crenshaw family was avid recyclers. I kid you not, from floor to ceiling, there were thousands of Miller Lite beer cans. It smelled like a brewery. I could only think of the well-catered bonfire we would have that year if I could cash in all these cans for the BBQ. The other two bedrooms were in as bad a shape as the rest of the house. Feeling horrible for the three boys growing up in this environment, it made me wonder if they even have a chance at a normal life. Months later and I was still getting the lot rent for the Crenshaw junk-storage building.

Update: A year and a half later, I got tired of seeing the POS double-wide junking up space number 1. I had always thought of this space as the gateway to our park because it was right at the entrance to the park. With the deck falling down, windows broken, doors falling off the hinges, and being filthy from the sap of trees, *it had to go!* I contacted Tom, and we agreed that he get off his butt and get the home cleaned out and ready to sell. (*Good luck with that,* I thought.)

By lying to him that I had another trailer ready to go into space number 1, I put a bit of a fire under said butt. Two months later and two more full dumpsters hauled to the dump, he found a buyer.

I can only hope that their new residence will not end up in the same condition, and now the gateway to our park looks a lot more appealing.

CHAPTER 12

Cops

Being in the type of business we have for over forty years, one can expect to have a certain amount of contact with law enforcement. We have—even with my strict rules to prevent such a thing from happening. Rule number 3 clearly states, the privacy of others should always be respected. Loud parties, music, TV, traffic, fighting, illegal activity, and *police calls* will not be tolerated. It goes on to say, if you have a problem with a neighbor, please call me immediately. After all, I am the cop of the park!

To back this statement, I will say that I am a graduate of the Citizen Police Academy. This is an eight-week course that the City Police Department offers to citizens interested in learning the ins and outs of local law enforcement. We were schooled in the areas of basic law, rights of citizens, dispatch, identification of illegal narcotics, use of weapons, target practice, and simulated situations. We also learned the meaning of the thin blue line. If you want to know what it means, you will just have to take the course. Finally, I've taken the concealed weapons course many times and have carried a weapon since the mideighties.

With all my training and much common sense, I came up with what I thought were very simple and easy-to-follow rules of the park.

So let's see how *that* plan worked out.

A major offender of *all* my rules was a woman in her thirties with a bit of an odd behavior about her, but I decided to give her a shot at renting from us anyway. Huge mistake!

On the first night Monica stayed with us in unit number 29, the sheriff's department was called three times for assistance. The first time deputies responded was because Monica's boyfriend got rough with her. The second time was because Monica beat the crap out of the boyfriend. Call number three we still can't figure out because no one answered the door after the cops arrived.

The next day, I confronted Ms. Monica about breaking rule number 3 and told her this was not a normal occurrence in the park. She assured me that the situation was under control, and we would not see her boyfriend again because he was entering a treatment program. This never happened. In the next week, I personally dialed 911 five times for various reasons, *all* emanating from unit number 29. And twice the police were called by her with accusations against *me*!

The first of five times I called was for all the traffic coming and going around number 29. When I got there, I witnessed six cars parked in the yard around Monica's place. Going to the door and letting myself in, I saw multiple people in each room. I also witnessed drug paraphernalia in plain view. Used needles and burnt spoons were on the counter in the kitchen. I also saw stacks of electronics and jewelry plus a huge pile of what looked like watches that had been taken apart. In the time it took the first sheriff's department vehicle to show up, all the drug stuff and what I assumed to be hot items mysteriously disappeared. The few stragglers who remained were asked to leave and warned not to come back or face trespassing charges.

The warning of no trespass was ignored the next day when I saw many of the same cars that were there the previous day along with several others, again parked all over the yard of number 29. This time I printed up a thirty-day notice to quit and then called the cops. When they got there, I handed Ms. Monica the eviction notice, and the deputies cleared the house of unwanted guests. My tenant acted all surprised that I had her friends chased off. I explained to her that ours was a family park, and if she wanted to party all day long, maybe she should find another place to do it. Of course, with the thirty-day notice in hand, she felt like she had a month to do whatever the hell she wanted.

I didn't see it that way. So the next day I conducted an emergency inspection (I smelled gas). Walking through the house, I found two guys in the front bedroom dug in like ticks. They told me that Monica was letting them live there. I told them that wasn't the deal I worked with Monica. I then dialed 911. Deputies came and escorted the pair off the property.

Later that day, I was paid a visit from the sheriff's department. It was explained to me that when Monica got home, she found I had changed the locks (which is against the law) and was harassing her by kicking out her friends. The truth was, Monica had lost the keys to the house on first day of her stay after I told her I didn't have copies of the keys. I also had given her $5 to get copies made and get them back to me (never happened). When the two friends were asked to leave, they must have locked the doors from the inside, essentially locking Monica out. With a pry bar and a screwdriver, I broke into the house, letting Ms. Monica back into her flophouse.

Several more visits were made by law enforcement before my wife and I left for a much-needed vacation. The thirty-day eviction would expire while we were away, so we were hoping our troubles would be gone when we got back… They weren't!

When we were picked up at the airport by a tenant (who was also my handyman), it took him the whole trip home to explain to us what had gone on while we were out of town. He said that the traffic actually picked up with loud, wild parties day and night. The yard was a mess with beer cans strewn everywhere, and the electricity was turned off. But the worst thing to me was when we were told that a dog was heard barking in the house all hours of the day and night. I was livid.

When we got home at midnight, the first thing I did was to grab my .380, a flashlight, and a headlamp from our house and then went straight to number 29. Bursting in the door of the rental, I first saw a guy on the living room floor, taking watches apart using a flashlight for illumination. He started yelling, "Monica, manager! Monica, manager!"

I rushed down the hall to the master bedroom, where I found Monica and her boyfriend in bed with a pit bull puppy between them. First thing I said was, "Monica, it's checkout time." Looking around the room, I saw dog shit everywhere. Its feet had never touched grass. I then told her the dog was leaving right now.

She started screaming, "What dog? Ain't got no dog!"

So I grabbed up the canine and started toward the door when I was blocked by Mr. Boyfriend. He said that it was his dog and, "It wasn't going nowhere."

I shoved it in his chest and told him to get rid of it now, "or else," and he agreed.

Monica started yelling, "Ain't got no court date! Ain't got no court date!" and "Illegal entry, illegal entry!"

As I made my way to the door, I stated loudly, "If you have anything in here you value, you best get it out quick." I then said, "I'll be starting a renovation in the morning."

Monica was screaming, "No renovation, no renovation!"

The next day, when they were gone, I backed my sixteen-foot flatbed trailer up to unit number 29 and, with the help of two tenants, loaded everything from the house to the trailer. The day after that, I learned the location of a friend of theirs and took all the crap and unloaded it onto the front yard. I call this my one-hour eviction and have used it several times over the years. It's probably very illegal, but I have not heard a peep from Ms. Monica or any of her druggie friends.

Below is a list of rules I've had in place for the entirety of my career.

1. Rent is due the first of the month. (Monica was only with us for three months. She was very late with rent the second month and never paid for the third.)

2. All utilities are the renter's responsibility. (She never had the gas turned on, so she never had heat during the coldest months of the year. I loaded three kerosene-burning heaters on the trailer during the one-hour eviction.)

3. The privacy of others should always be respected. Loud parties, music, TV, traffic, fights, illegal activity, and police calls will not be tolerated. (This rule was blown all to hell!)

4. Homes will be kept clean and in good repair. (I can show pictures that I took during the eviction that looked like animals had lived in the home. Oh yeah, they had.)

5. Each renter is expected to keep the premises (exterior) neat and clean. (Beer cans and garbage filled the yard.)

6. Absolutely no pets. (There was the pit bull dog. Now we have always had a dog in our household, and when I am challenged by this fact and asked, "Why can you have a dog and we can't?" I inevitably come back with, "You go purchase sixteen acres like I did, then you can make up your own rules.")

7. Garbage pickup is once a week, on Tuesday. Recycling is mandatory. (The storage building I offered her was full from floor to ceiling with three months of garbage. They did not separate recyclables.)

8. To receive full return of deposit, the home must be clean and in good repair, and a thirty-day notice to vacate must be given to management. All abandoned items will become

property of management. (The house was a mess, and there was damage in every room.)

This bitch was a landlord's nightmare. In forty-plus years of mobile home park management, there was never a tenant who broke *every* one of my simple rules until... *Monica*.

The only bright spot from all the extracurricular activities this horrible person brought to our little community was all the fine people we met working for the county. Thank you, Garland County Sheriff's Department, for the many responses and professional manner in which each incident was handled at all hours of the day and night. We are so glad they are there when we need them.

A siren sounds in the middle of the night. I listen as the wailing gets closer and closer. Suddenly, when it's at its loudest, the siren stops. This scenario usually means that there is some kind of trouble in the park. Jumping out of bed and donning my emergency night-time uniform, I race to my truck. The flashing blue lights tell me in what direction I need to go to find the trouble.

When I discover that the lights are atop the cars of *state* troopers, I brace myself for a more advanced situation than the usual domestic disturbance, which is handled by the *county* law enforcement.

Flagging down the responding state officers, I introduce myself as owner of the park and offer my assistance. I am told by a female officer that one of my tenants, a convicted felon on parole, has been in a high-speed chase with her. She is extremely motivated to locate my eluding renter and gives me his name and several aliases. I recognize the name, Dennis, as a relatively new tenant who had moved into unit number 26 with his wife, old lady, or girlfriend (not sure which she was). The same day Dennis's brother had moved in with his family, choosing number 2 to make their home.

With this information, the troopers went first to unit number 26 with no luck finding Dennis. I suggested looking at unit number 2 since the brothers spent much time between the two trailers. Bingo!

With officers on each side of the home, the female trooper pounded on the front door. Mr. Dennis immediately came flying out the back. Watching all the action from my truck, I could see the troopers were in hot pursuit of their prey, this time on foot. It looked to me that Dennis was making his way back to his home, number 26, and probably would have made it. But just as he was about to run behind my truck, I slammed it into reverse and hit the gas.

Dennis ran full speed into the back quarter panel of my vehicle, then collapsed to the ground. I got out and convinced him that the chase was over, and he best give up before he got hurt any worse. He agreed. Seconds later, the troopers were hooking up the handcuffs and escorting Dennis off the property to his next residence.

Before leaving, the lady trooper thanked me for the help, saying she had never seen a better takedown of a suspect by using a vehicle. She said it was textbook, but next time, I should leave it to the professionals. Well…not quite… What she actually said to me was, "What in the hell do you think you're doing, interfering with official law enforcement business?" and "Hopefully the prisoner will sue you for assault." Ungrateful bitch! I find that county deputies are much easier to work with than state troopers.

Ten years later, a semifamiliar face showed up at our door. It was Dennis—sporting numerous prison tattoos. He just wanted to tell me that he was getting his life together and thanked me for his short time spent in the park and my assistance in starting him toward a better direction.

Good luck, Dennis, I know you can make it by making positive life choices.

The response time of law enforcement to a call for assistance will usually be determined by the urgency of the situation. The time it takes for help to arrive often seems forever, especially if you happen to be the one who made the call to 911.

The fastest response to an emergency call was made on a tenant who was a repeat offender. My request to 911 went as follows.

911 would ask, "What is your emergency?"

I replied, "This is Gary Strakshus, owner of Brundage Woods Mobile Home Park at 108 Old Brundage Road." I have made enough calls to this number and watched plenty of cop shows on TV, so I know how to get right down to the meat of what the dispatch person needs to hear. I continued, "There is an attractive, naked blonde female running through the trailer park, breaking windows, and kicking in doors." (You might recall that Sarah's story is also in chapter 3, told from a different perspective.)

I knew that ought to do it. Within minutes, three county units were on the scene, putting Sarah in the back of one of the cars. The deputies seemed very disappointed that I had wrapped the offender in a huge beach towel before they got there.

The second fastest response was a call I made one week later. I said, "There is an attractive blonde female wearing a skimpy bikini, walking down the middle of the highway and stopping traffic." Once again deputies were on scene double-quick, scooping up Sarah and hauling her off to jail.

Another way to get responders quickly to the location of the emergency is to report an extremely tall black male with a machete, threatening to use it on a Vietnamese family. This call was made one fine Fourth of July, before my "no fireworks in the park" policy was put into place.

Early in the evening, families had begun the tradition of shooting off their fireworks, bottle rockets, Roman candles, and sparklers. One family, who happened to be of Vietnamese descent, was shooting bottle rockets up the hill in the direction of unit number 9. My renter in number 9, who was a very large black man, claimed to be a Vietnam war vet with PTSD. (It turns out Dutch was younger than me, and I was too young for that war.)

Anyway, he went nuts, claiming the Viet Cong were trying to kill him with their mortars coming down on his location. I got a call from the Asian family that Dutch was threatening them with a knife. Actually it was a two-foot machete, and the lunatic was swinging it at the gooks, that is, anyone with yellow skin color.

I made the call to 911, and the response time was impressive, possibly saving lives. Three cops surrounded the madman, who had to be tazed and maced before he could be put in handcuffs and tossed in the back of the county unit. Peace was brought back to the community, and I immediately issued a *"no fireworks"* policy, which stands to this day.

An unexpected contact with police happened while I was cutting the grass in the park. While making my way mowing around the homes, I noticed an unfamiliar vehicle circling the trailer park. On its next loop, I witnessed what looked to be an unmarked police car right behind it. Then a county deputy's unit pulled to a stop right in front of the unidentified, suspicious automobile, causing it to be pinned between the two officers. I just love this stuff.

Watching from the seat of my mower, real-life drama was occurring right in front of me. With guns drawn, the cops ordered the driver out of his vehicle. He refused to comply, which turned out to be a big mistake on his part. The deputies gently assisted the guy out of his car, and somehow he ended up facedown on the ground, with dirt in his mouth and hands cuffed behind his back. The whole time the knucklehead was cussing and screaming threats at the sheriff deputies.

Past experience and watching cop shows has taught me not to interfere with official police business, but I can't help myself. I asked the undercover cop, "What's up?" He informed me that he had been patrolling the area when he spotted what he knew to be his uncle's stolen car. Running a background check on the guy spitting dirt, we found out he was a convicted felon with wants and warrants on him for theft, robbery, and assault. We could now add grand theft auto to his list of crimes with more to come after this investigation.

Now I was really getting into this! Taking inventory of the vehicle, we discovered bags full of wallets, credit cards, driver's licenses, jewelry, and drugs plus paraphernalia. In the trunk we found pistols, rifles, shotguns, and assorted ammo along with a bunch of knives. It was determined that this guy had been very busy since he had only been out of prison for a week.

Then he was yelling (and cussing), "You guys are gonna cause me to go back to prison!" He continued his yelling and cussing as the deputies carefully put him in the squad car. Then he looked right at me and asked, "You have a lovely trailer park. Do you have any rentals open?" When I began to laugh, he said, "Well, fuck you too!" At least this guy was consistent—he cussed all the way to the end.

The next day, the news of our arrest was on the front page of the local paper. The headline stated, "Traffic Stop on Suspicious Vehicle Leads to Felony Arrest." It was so great to be a part of getting a bad actor off the streets and sending him back to where he belongs.

Let's keep up the good work and be safe out there.

CHAPTER 13

Alzheimer's

In dealing with lots of people over many years, you can count on coming across people with the horrible affliction known as Alzheimer's disease.

Years ago, it was often called dementia, and it was every bit as horrible. I believe my first encounter with someone with dementia was in 1977 when I took charge of our first mobile home park. Ray Favorite, who you met in chapter 1, was an old man in number 2 who told me he was in the Army with Henry Mancini. When I told him I didn't believe him, he showed me a picture of two Army guys in full gas mask outfits. He then pointed at one of the men and said, "That's me and the other guy is Henry Mancini." After Ray did a bunch of other goofy stuff, including dating my grandmother, I gave my first "diagnosis" of dementia.

Another old renter with the same ailment was Monk Melton, who you also met in chapter 1. It was very sad for me to watch Monk slip into the grip of the disease. He was not only a renter but also a friend who took me fishing every week. The old man's condition got to be very bad, but he refused to quit driving. The problem was Monk would leave the park in the morning in his boat of a Cadillac to go to the store, but he couldn't, for the life of him, find his way home. It got so bad that I had to put a handwritten note in the Caddy, which read, "If found, please return to 401 Lakeland Drive, number 14." After local law enforcement actually did just that a few times, they took the keys to the car away from my friend. Soon thereafter, Monk was placed in a nursing home, where he wasted away to nothing.

The only thing worse than having a good friend or tenant fall to this unspeakable illness would be to have a relative end up with it. When my mother began to forget things and couldn't express her thoughts and needs without getting very upset, we knew something was up.

For over ten years, my father was the sole home care provider for my mother. My wife Gay and I did what we could but could see that caring for Mom was killing my dad. My waste-of-time sister moved in with them under the pretense of caring for them both, but after one year, we had to remove her from the home…by force.

Late one night, my dad called me and said he needed me to come to his house and get my sister, Gayle, out as soon as I could. Thirty minutes later, I was told by my father that my sister had been abusing him for a year. He showed me cuts from her fingernails on both arms. I went straight to her door and knocked, saying, "Gayle, it's checkout time. Your services are no longer needed, and you are not wanted here."

She went apeshit crazy, so I called the police and emergency medical for Dad's wounds. The cops came and kicked my sister back to her house, which my father had given her in my mobile home park. EMTs examined and treated Dad's wounds.

While this was all going on, Mom was freaking out from all the stimulation of extra activity. She was a mess for hours before she calmed down. My wife and I had a sit-down family talk with Dad the next day and convinced him that it was time to place Mom in a caring home. We had been urging this for over a year, but it took this blowup to finally make Dad realize we were right.

We decided on a wonderful home just down the street from us. There are only three residents and twenty-four-hour care. The caretakers are very nice, and Mom seems to like them. Of course, when I visit, she doesn't know who I am and sometimes is very nasty to me. When I stopped by on Mother's Day, she told me to "get the hell out of here." Same results when I came for her birthday celebration. So instead of upsetting her, I stay away most of the time. It's like she is a totally different person from the mother that raised me.

This illness is the worst!

Karen Mc was a sweet lady who retired from her job with the City of Hot Springs Water Department. She actually rented from us two separate times. The first was in her own small two-bedroom home located at number 18. She lived in it for many years, but when her mother died, Karen moved into her mother's home. Years later, Karen bought another mobile home, a sixteen-by-eighty three-bedroom, two-bath, beautiful monster of a home. She didn't need a house that big, but she wanted it and was very happy in it. Her long-time companion was a four-legged rascal named Shelby. Shelby was a cute Jack Russell terrier, and they were inseparable.

But when Karen started walking the park with her dog and wearing a pith helmet, long rubber gloves, a face mask, and clunky army boots, I began to wonder if she was beginning to slip into the dark pit of Alzheimer's. Soon she was calling me from dollar stores, saying she had lost her keys or wallet and needed help to find them.

Inevitably, I would rush to her location and immediately would look in her purse and find the missing item.

I have previously mentioned that we are a full-service mobile home park, and I am happy to help my people in any way I can. But with the increased occurrences of bailing Ms. Karen out of her absent-minded trips around town, I began to worry that I was going to lose another victim of the disease. I was correct.

In no time her sister and brother-in-law placed Karen in a nursing home without much chance of coming back to her home with us. Gay and I would visit Ms. Karen about once a month, and when we were interacting with her, she seemed to be happy and well cared for. As time went on, however, we noticed that she was less in the moment and reliving the past memories she had. The disease had sucked her soul, personality, and health right out of her.

Another single lady who also lived with us two separate times was Jean T. The original time Jean was a part of our park was when we were just up and running. Ms. T's was the second home to be moved into our brand-new park. She chose space number 2 for her older model, a fourteen-by-seventy mobile home. Jean worked at the Club Café restaurant in downtown Hot Springs. The café was a favorite of the local crowd and in the old days served many famous folks, including the family of Bill Clinton. Jean was a fixture in the place, serving tables from the day the place opened to its last day of existence.

With her hair piled on top of her head, a pink-and-white dress, the high-heeled shoes, and, of course, her thick Southern accent, we just naturally called her Flo. (Flo was the name of waitress in an old TV show, which took place in an old-time café, for those too young to remember.) Flo's first stint with us lasted a few years and was uneventful.

The only strange thing I can remember about Jean during this time was she tried to bring a dead stick to life from her yard by putting it into a pot of dirt and watering it daily. She was very persistent, but the dead stick never did sprout a leaf. Soon after, she moved.

We didn't see her again once she left the park until one day, thirty years later, Jean showed up at our door looking for a rental. I happened to have a one-bedroom, and she fell in love with it. Unit number 3 is an older model, one-bedroom, one-bath, and it was just perfect for our Ms. Jean. The day she signed the lease, a friend of hers came with her to assist her in the transaction. We never saw the lady again once the lease was signed.

It was almost like she was dumping Jean on us. Soon it became obvious to us that that was exactly what had happened. When I asked Jean if she had any furniture, Jean replied she didn't know. When I asked her if she got the utilities in her name, she said she thought so. Pressing further, I asked about transportation, and she said she had a nice truck. It took a few days of investigating, but I finally determined that the last place Jean laid her head was about ten miles down the road in a shack of a house…that to me…should have been burned to the ground. Carefully climbing the front porch to avoid it falling down and killing myself, I made it to the front door, which was off its hinges.

Peering inside revealed a horrific sight. If you are familiar the TV show *Hoarders*, you can imagine what I was looking at—filthy crap from floor to ceiling of boxes, crates, bags full of who knows what, and nasty furniture I wouldn't let my dog on. This is funny because there were half a dozen four-legged critters on couches, chairs, and beds. When I asked Jean about the animals, she said people dropped them off for her. She also said at night she got cats and coons that came in looking for a handout. By the amount of dog, cat, and coon poop, this had been going on for a prolonged period of time.

It was then that I thought of looking for the nice truck Jean had told me about. Exiting out the way I had come in, I began to explore the property with all the vines, overgrown weeds, and downed, dead trees. It was tough going. Then there it was, in an old, decrepit lean-to. I couldn't believe my eyes. Jean had a brand-new, cherry-red, jacked-up Ford pickup. And the keys were in it!

My mission was clear. I cleared a trail from the truck storage to the house and from the house to the road. I began loading the truck with stuff Jean would need and headed with it to her new home in her beautiful truck. Have I mentioned we are a full-service mobile home park? It took three days and countless loads in my truck and sixteen-foot flatbed trailer, but we got Jean relocated, leaving the most disgusting junk back at her old habitat. The whole time I was wondering, *What am I getting myself into?* But we loved our old TV friend and waitress, Flo. So I wasn't giving up on her *just yet*!

We assisted in getting the utilities turned on in her name, and Jean cleared a path through the house between all her boxes and treasures to the bedroom. Soon Jean was calling me every day, stating that things were missing. I would explain to her that the item in question was probably in one of the unopened boxes piled in the trailer, also assuring her that nobody would want her picture frames or knickknacks or whatever.

The day of our friend's diagnosis of Alzheimer's (by me) came when she called me to the house to talk. When I got to number 3, Jean was waiting for me, fully clothed and mad. The problem was, she was sitting there with underwear over her clothes. That's right— bra and panties on the outside. Before I could say anything, Jean accused me of being the one taking her things and that she wanted her box of Raisin Bran back "right now!"

She went on to say that she knew I was a thief, and the sheriff's department was on the way to take me to jail. Deputies did indeed arrive to see Jean making her fashion statement and listened to her complaint. They did a search of the place and found a box of Raisin Bran on top of the refrigerator and $3,500 in cash in her purse. She said the cereal and money weren't hers and didn't know how it got there.

Although this all was great fun and fantastic material for my book, I knew Jean was in trouble and needed help. I was able to locate her son, who lived in the area, but had drifted from his mother when she started to…lose it! We were able to locate a caring home that would take her, and the son cleaned out her stuff from number 3.

We will miss you, Flo.

CHAPTER 14

Kids

The first ten years of my career as a mobile home park owner and manager dealt with residents all over the age of eighty. A geriatric community indeed has its own special needs, spending extra time explaining that their grass will be cut or their leaves will be raked, or since I am washing my car, I will, of course, do theirs as well just as soon as I can. I really didn't mind these requests as most went toward the improvement of the park. And when each job was complete, my people were grateful and content until the next request came up.

The complexity and personality of the park changed when we began to rent to families with children. The high energy and activity of young people brought an end to the slow, quiet feeling of past days with my old folks. Soon kids were running all over the place, getting into stuff and situations, which I would inevitably have to deal with.

Debra M. was a single mother with two teenage daughters. The three moved into our relatively new "family park" and made their home in unit number 13. The younger of the two young girls was a bit mentally challenged and totally boy crazy. This proved to be a bad combination because soon every boy in the neighborhood came sniffing around for Debra's daughter. When I began to find used condoms in the upper section of my barn, I had a good idea where they were coming from and who at least half of the party had used them.

I enlisted several tenants to keep an eye on the barn for any extracurricular activities and soon got a report from one of my spies. Debra's young daughter was witnessed climbing the stairs to my barn, hand in hand with an off-campus local kid. A short time later, the pair came back down the stairs and went on their way.

Looking into this report, I found yet another used prophylactic. When I confronted Mom, she was adamant that her baby could not possibly have anything to do with it. Explaining to the single mother over and over what had been reported to me by my snitch, she was having none of it. A very short time later, we found that both daughters were pregnant, and they moved out.

One week after the three moved, a tenant (my snitch) witnessed the same young boy who had climbed the stairs with the youngest daughter skulking around the property. The kid was seen trying to set fire to my barn. I have always felt the reason this young boy was starting out his life as an arsonist was he thought he was getting even with me for ending his nooky sessions. Thankfully my eye guy stopped him and sent him on his way.

Nothing like this had ever happened when it was just my old people. I believe that's because none of them could climb the stairs.

I will admit that there was a good amount of trailer hopping by the old geezers, but this chapter is about children, so…

The absolute worst kids I ever had to deal with were being raised by a tenant who I had used for a time as my handyman; this is Todd, who you met in chapter 10. Todd had taken on the task of raising three very young boys who were the biological sons of an ex-girlfriend. Each boy was a product of different lovers. I felt very sorry for Todd and threw him as much work as I could, which consisted of carpentry, plumbing, electrical, and yard work. Each task was completed efficiently and quickly. The guy was talented.

However, the thing he didn't have a single clue about was parenting. The mother of the boys was doing time in prison after being found guilty on drug-related charges. The kids really didn't have much of a chance at a normal, healthy life. Todd was in way over his head, but he truly loved the little devils. Try as he might, it was obvious this was a family in deep trouble. In addition to his lack of parenting skills, my handyman did not have a vehicle or a driver's license. Being immobile meant the kids were stuck on location, allowing them to get into as much mischief as they could find. While other children were attending after-school activities, Todd's boys were terrorizing the trailer park.

Their amount of destruction began at a low level, with littering, breaking windows, and tearing up planting areas of other residents of the park. Complaints began flowing in, and I would confront Todd, hoping he would get each situation under control.

One means of punishment was for them to haul the family's garbage to the dumpster. The next day I would find the trash from number 13, Todd's unit, strewn over one acre on the back side of our property. It looked as if we had been hit by a tornado. Actually, we were the victims of three whirling dervishes.

It was easy for me to identify where the mess had originated by finding school homework with the boys' names on it. All the assignments that were graded by the teachers had big red Fs at the top. In addition to the school papers, there was the usual household garbage: empty pizza boxes, TV dinner containers, milk jugs, soup cans, soda bottles, and more ramen noodle boxes than I could count. The lack of a proper diet was evident.

There were also many empty prescription bottles with the boys' names on them. I really didn't want to see them when they were off their meds! Anyway, the wannabe father was notified about the mess, and he cleaned it up.

Another time, I caught the trio in the act of filling sewer access cleanouts with rocks. This is not good for the flow of septic. Todd dug up the lines and replaced them. Did I mention that he is an excellent handyman? The problem was Todd was spending most of his time fixing, repairing, and replacing damage that was done by his three masters of mayhem.

The older the boys got, the greater the offenses became. When residents began to report items missing, I knew we had a problem, and the first place I looked was to unit number 13. Doing a walk-through of Todd's home under the pretense of a safety inspection, what I found in the boys' room was very disturbing. TVs, PlayStations, DVDs, VCRs, jewelry, bicycles, and cigarettes were all in the small room. These kids were preteen, but it looked as if they were starting up a pawnshop. When I dropped the bombshell of evidence against his ambitious boys, all I got back from Todd was, "Boys will be boys."

It was then that I thought I might be the one over my head. I gave Todd the alternative to shape up or ship out. The stolen items were returned, and it seemed things got better. A month later, I was contacted by the state police that a complaint was filed against three young boys playing chicken with passing vehicles on the busy road bordering our property. Several cars actually ran off the road trying to avoid killing the kids. I had had enough. A thirty-day notice was given to Todd and his tribe, permitting them to stay till the end of the school year. After they left, peace and serenity suddenly were once again brought to the trailer park. I am not kidding. Immediately upon their departure, the personality of the park changed to a place of great calm. For a time I really missed my handy guy, having to do repairs myself. But the decision to rid ourselves of the terrible three-some was the right one.

Some of my tenants stayed in touch with Todd and the boys, and a few years later, the news was not good but predictable. The now teenagers were all in juvenile detention for crimes committed at their new location. Good luck, Todd, you'll need it.

Not all trailer-park kids are bad. In fact, most children with responsible and caring parents end up turning out just great. Two such success stories are a pair of girls growing up in very different families just about next to each other in the park.

Ann Marie is a cute, energetic little ball of fire and a bit of a tomboy but definitely all girl. Her mother is a gymnastic coach, photographer, and devoted supporter of her daughter's activities. Ann Marie's father is a hardworking employee of the local cable company and the son of one of our longest residents. Dad Cody did a good bit of his growing up in our community, and after getting married to his wife, Heaven, they decided to make their home with us in unit number 26.

Two doors down from them in number 28 is the Rodríguez family—Frank and Sara being the parents of three children, two boys and a girl. The eldest is Anna, the sweetest, kindest, and most talented little person on the face of the earth. Her father, Frank, also my current handyman, is of Mexican descent. He is a huge man and did ten years in prison on drug charges. His prison tats and size cause him to be a very imposing subject, but he has been nothing but kind, thoughtful, and caring to us and others in the park. I must say that Frank is also the best handyman I have ever had. Mother Sara is a dedicated little lady who keeps her family in line. The two preteen girls are best of friends and, when they are both in the park, are inseparable.

Ann Marie was first to enter the world of beauty pageants. The success she had was not only local but national as well. She would come to me and tell me where her next competition would be, dressed in her newest gown or costume, and then do her walk or strut to music. I would, of course, give her a contribution as her sponsor, and when she won, she would bring her trophy for me to see. It was all very exciting, and Ann Marie not only loved it but was also very good at playing the role of beauty queen.

All this excitement did not go unnoticed by bestie Anna. Soon she was coming to our house in her new outfit, makeup and all, doing her routine for our judgment. In a very short time, Anna was winning each event she entered. She was a natural, and I, of course, became her sponsor as well.

As a part of the competitions, the girls were to participate in some sort of community service. The mothers of the queens would come to me with ideas of things the girls could do to benefit the park or its residents. Some of the ideas included picking up trash, hauling the trash and recyclables for the people of the park, raking yards, having a lemonade stand on the corner, and holding an Easter egg hunt for the kids of the park. The girls would keep track of their time spent with each event and document the details and how much was collected in donations. With each pageant, our mobile home park was a great benefactor, and the little ladies learned life lessons.

I only wish there were pageants for little boys.

I'm not sure what the statistics are for autistic children versus normal kids, but I'm thinking we are way above the norm for having special children in our park. Out of the dozen or so kids in the park, at least half are afflicted with a form of autism. I have no idea what to attribute this fact, but it is very perplexing.

Jake M. and his family have lived in the park since he was an infant. He is high functioning and does attend public school. This kid has the greatest imagination I have ever encountered. Every person who comes within eye contact with Jake is welcomed with a "Hey, I've got to tell you something." He then begins to ramble on about an imaginary story, usually with something about *Harry Potter* or some *Star Wars* characters. His mind will spew out situations and stories for hours if his mother lets him, but she will cut him short when she sees the eyes of his captives beginning to roll back in their head.

Another fact is that Jake is the spitting image of Harry Potter. I kid you not—on Halloween when he dresses as young Harry with the scar on his forehead, his cape, his wand, and, of course, the round-rim Harry eyeglasses, you think he is going to cast a spell on you! You've just got to love him.

One Christmas, the volunteer fire department came through the park as they do each year, with Santa handing out candy canes for the kids. They made their way around the park with music and sirens blaring, visiting with each child who would come out of their homes. I visited with the chief, who had lived in the park years ago, thanked him and the guys, and sent them to their next stop.

Walking home, I noticed Jake in front of his house singing and dancing…all excited…as he can get. I asked if he had seen Santa, knowing the trucks had been around the park twice. He said, "Not yet!" So I ducked behind a trailer and quick made a call to our former tenant and chief to see if they could come back and visit a child who had been missed. They were happy to find a place to turn the trucks around and head back to Jake. Two of the trucks were *ladder* trucks!

When they pulled up in front of Jake's house, I thought he was going to explode with excitement. Santa jumped down from the truck and gave him a big hug. That was it. I told the chief they were going to be there a while. Sure enough, Jake started in on some fantastic fantasy about walking, talking robot snowmen who were going to take over the planet. The firemen stayed until they got an emergency call and had to leave.

Many of our collection of autistic children are too young for us to know just how they are going to turn out. One child, whom I will call Z, was from a family with three kids. Two of the three were diagnosed with autism. The diagnosis, of course, was made by me.

For years I would tell the parents about the wonderful schools in the area that would accommodate and truly assist the needs of Z. This was directed to deaf ears. When Z turned five years old and was still making only animal noises, the parents finally looked into an alternative school. Z and his young brother are now making great progress in First Step School for special children.

CHAPTER 15

The Final Chapter
(Maybe)

So I was wondering how to bring this story to a close. What could be more final than the subject of death.

Many people will say that death is a part of life. I believe that death is the end of life as we know it. Although we have seen many births bringing new life to young residents of our park, the deaths far outnumber them. Just off the top of my head, I would guess a ratio of ten-to-one vis-à-vis deaths to births. Of course, all the tenants from our first park are long departed.

When you purchase a trailer park with nothing but eighty-year-old-plus folks, you've got to expect that. It seems like a lifetime ago, but I can still remember each renter who lived with us and is now gone. Here are those from our first park.

In Remembrance

- Ray Favorite: Retired sign painter, dated my grandmother, and spent time in the service during WWI, allegedly alongside Henry Mancini. More of his story is in chapters 1 and 13.
- Margret Von Bargen: Never seemed to be happy. Always asked me to wash her car when she saw me washing mine. Repaid me with pastries.
- Ruby Hess: Mother of my mother and dated Ray Favorite. We never got along.
- Dallas Lynch: Lived in Little Rock but spent weekends with us. In the fall, he would rake his yard area, filling tarps and calling them canoes. "I filled five canoes today," he would tell me.
- Murial and Austin Seacrest: Buried them both in the lake just offshore from where they had lived for many years. Their story is in chapter 1.
- Dorothy and Mr. Kelly: Never knew his name because he always went by Kelly. He spent his life as a bookie on the horses that run out of the local racetrack. Kelly was never off the phone or seen without a strong drink in his hand. His wife, Dorothy, was a saint!
- Ray Gideonson: Retired mobile home park owner. Ray started most conversations with "I don't mean to tell you how to run your business, but…" Then he'd tell me how!
- Al Kostrick and wife, Alberta: Al was the one-armed fisherman who died choking on his vomit after drinking at the racetrack all day. Alberta watched as I tried to resuscitate

him, breaking ribs in the process. You read their story in chapter 1.

- Ted Mills: Ted died of alcohol poisoning, which was poured down his throat by Alice "Black Widow" Cates. This terrible tale is also fully told in chapter 1.

- Lou Brinkman: Very nice man who developed what is known as floppy feet syndrome. We could hear him walking past our house each day slapping his huge, duck-like feet on the walkway to the boat dock. A good fisherman.

- Cecil Willingham: He and his girlfriend, Gladys Selvedge, were the managers of the park before I took over. I don't think they ever liked me but were always quick to say, "I don't mean to tell you how to run your business, but…" Gladys was also found naked, passed out in the yard, the first week I took over their jobs.

- Harry Able: Nicest and kindest man, who fished each day and never caught a fish.

- Harold Hilliard: Only man to catch fewer fish than Mr. Able. Owned a boat for one day and died of a huge growth on his head. The stories of both these fishermen are in chapter 1.

- Mr. and Mrs. Montgomery: Knew very little about them but liked them very much. Remember them telling me to wait as long as possible to cut the grass in the spring. I'm not sure why, but that tidbit has stuck with me for forty years.

- Mr. Parmenter or Mr. Periwinkle, as my wife and I knew him: Insisted on having a planting area around his trailer hitch at the front of his home. Years later, when I bought his home and was going to move it to our new park, we found that the hitch had rotted away to nothing due to the dirt in the garden. I had to purchase a new hitch and have it welded to the home.

- James "Monk" Melton: Sweet old man who taught me all I know about fishing. He was the first person I knew who died of Alzheimer's. Monk claimed to be of American

Indian descent and always had a piece of his lunch on his upper lip. His full story is told in chapters 1 and 13.

- John Skeya: John was not only a tenant but also a friend and mentor. He taught me much about plumbing, electrical, carpentry, and working sheet metal. He died in the hospital with me holding his hand, telling him we would soon float and fish a river when we both knew that was not to be. I miss my friend John.

That concludes most of the deaths of our folks who lived with us in our first mobile home park. Most of the deaths were age-related because most of the people were in their eighties or older.

Our second business was a bit further out of town, so we accommodated young singles, young families, and retired folks. The ages of our renters pretty much eliminated age-related death. But the young can be very creative when it comes to their demise. When I think of it, there are probably over a hundred ways to die in a trailer park. Included on the list would be illness, accident, drugs, broken heart, suicide, and murder. I'm sorry to say that our second mobile home park has seen the death of tenants by *all* these possible ways.

A sad but very impactful death was the one of Al Roy. Al was the property owner of the sixteen acres I fell in love with and wanted to develop. It wasn't for sale, but I visited with Al and kept showing him I was very interested in his property.

Al had run a few cattle years previous but had let the place run down and become overgrown. The front eight acres had a gentle slope and a mixture of oaks, pines, and a small pond. He lived in a dilapidated, hundred-year-old house with his girlfriend and her two kids. I never told Al what I had in mind for the acreage, but I would show up at his place just about quarterly to show I was still interested. Oftentimes on my visits, I would not even mention my intentions but help him with a project he had procrastinated doing because of his age and physical limitations.

All the time, behind Al's back I was imagining the layout for my beautiful little mobile home park. I felt a bit bad not being honest with the old-timer, so after about two years of marinating him, I told Al that I would like to develop a few trailer spaces and move my entire family to the place. I even shot him a price of $4,500 per acre for the front eight, which was top dollar in the mid-1980s.

About the same time, Al told me he was approached by investors who wanted to develop the same piece of land. Their intention was to build a rubber band factory! Totally repulsed by that idea, Al agreed to sell to me, and the deal was done. I immediately began clearing for mobile homes, and Al remodeled his old house with the money I gave him for the property.

Within six months, Al became very ill and was hospitalized, having been diagnosed with terminal cancer. Al died in his hospital bed during one of my visits with only me in his room. He never got to see my dream come true of a nice mobile home park on what was once his property.

After he died, I bought the back eight acres at an auction that his family was holding to liquidate and divvy up among them. If it weren't for the death of this sweet old man and my friend, we wouldn't have the business and beautiful home we've lived in for over thirty years.

Thank you, Al. I hope you are proud of me and what I have done with your place.

A siren sounds in the distance. Out of bed like a shot, I jump into my emergency nighttime clothes, which I keep by the bed (like the fireman that I'm not)…and listen. If the siren continues on, going down the road off into the night, I go back to sleep. If it cuts off suddenly anywhere near our property, I rush to my truck and head out to locate the emergency.

Finding flashing lights anywhere near our sixteen acres is never a good thing. One night, after hearing the sirens at about 2:30 a.m., I ran out looking for the emergency. I found it at space number 21. The unit had been rented out about thirty days prior to a young single mother of two. Jennifer Williams was an attractive young lady in her midtwenties with two of the cutest kids, ages four and 1 1/2 years old.

During the initial interview (see chapter 13 for the conversation), Jennifer happened to mention that she was going through a horrible divorce. When I asked her if her soon-to-be ex-husband would be a problem for her, she said, "Only if he finds us." Turns out, he did (allegedly).

In fact, Jennifer was packing boxes with her belongings, intending to move out that night. It was apparent she was house-hopping, trying to stay out of reach of her husband. Evidence showed that she was sitting at the kitchen table, having coffee with someone. (There were two cups.) The children had been put to bed, and there was a child gate in the doorway to their bedroom.

Jennifer's current boyfriend had been out drinking with his buddies and came to her house very late to check on her. He found her shot twice in the head. The boyfriend called the authorities, and that's when all the sirens began. When I got to number 21, police, ambulance, detectives, and eventually the coroner showed up on scene. Jennifer had been murdered.

After detectives processed the crime scene and everyone left, I knew it was time for me to pick up the pieces and get things back to normal. I assured all my tenants that this was not a random event and that it was in fact probably very personal. I also made clear that there was not somebody going around just shooting innocent people. Most tenants went out soon after and bought weapons anyway.

Then it was time to get the trailer in order and ready to rent. After all, that's what we do. (I found out much later there are companies that actually do a restoration after such a thing occurs…if only I had known.)

Entering the home was very unnerving. Two coffee cups on the table, chair overturned in the living room, and a pool of blood on the carpet. Upon further inspection, I found bloody baby fingerprints on the child gate to the kids' bedroom. Best I can figure is that the kids heard the shots, woke up, and climbed over the gate to get to their mother. They must have then climbed back over and gone to bed because that's where the police found them—covered with the blood of their mother.

No one was ever convicted of this murder, though many people knew who the person responsible for the crime was. (He was heard saying that if he couldn't have her, nobody could.) I only hope that Jennifer's two little boys somehow grew up to be healthy, normal young men if there is any way possible.

Ray Guidroz showed up at our home and office shortly after we started construction of our new park. He said he was interested in renting a small two-bedroom that needed to be very inexpensive. I had just moved in a trailer, which met his specs, to space number 3. I showed it to him, and he said it would do.

Ray was a bit rough to look at, being a throwback from the early seventies. He reminded me of the hippie movement with his long, dirty hair and nasty clothes, not to mention his large green Dodge van.

Ray fell into life at our park very comfortably, where we would oftentimes see him rolling and smoking joints on his front porch. I didn't know where he got the money to pay rent, but he was never late, always paying on the first of the month.

Then one day… Ray was *gone*. After staying with us for ten years, he just disappeared. Very strange. After three years, though, Ray showed up, wanting to rent from us again. I said we could do that especially since I had a small two-bedroom about the same vintage as the last one he had stayed in. My one condition was that he fill me in on his disappearance for three years. He agreed.

Ray began by telling me that thirteen years ago he was a member of the United States military. For the ten years he had stayed with us, he had been AWOL. He had hid out with us, looking over his shoulder the entire time. Ray had family in the area but was smart enough not to visit them at their homes. This was in case the government was looking for him. I mention the words "smart enough" because when Ray was given an IQ test, he was found to be at genius level.

Anyway, his life on the run got to him, and he decided to turn himself in and do the time. The three years he did in a Texas prison were not kind to him. He had aged considerably, and his health was that of a man twice his age. He spent the next ten years mostly on his front porch, smoking pot and drinking more whiskey than anyone should.

Then the calls and texts began to come in.

The first call for help came at 2:00 a.m. one weekday night. Not that it mattered to Ray because I'm sure to him, every day was a Saturday. Answering the phone, I learned from a distressed Ray that he needed help sitting up in bed so he could make his way to the bathroom. It seemed that his back and legs had quit working.

I rushed down to his trailer to find the most god-awful mess I had ever seen. Entering the house, I immediately saw a burned-out hole in the middle of the living room floor the size of a basketball. I could actually see the ground under the trailer. The rest of the house was a total disaster, and the smell was unbearable. I made my way to the back bedroom walking down the hall, which was covered in human waste.

I found Ray in the bed covered with more of the same. I helped Ray into a seated position, which was no easy task. Looking around the room, I was reminded of the conditions in which Howard Hughes was found in his latter days. Empty whiskey bottles, ashtrays over filled with cigarette butts, and used orange-juice bottles full of urine covered every inch of the room.

Ray said he had to pee, so I emptied an orange-juice bottle in the toilet and let him relieve himself. Tucking him in for the night, I told him I would check on him in the morning. The first thing I did when I got home was take a long hot shower. Then I lay in bed thinking about what my plan was for my poor tenant.

As the sun was just coming up in the eastern sky, I began to get calls and texts from Ray. I spent the entire morning running to his house to get him ice for his whiskey, roll him a joint, roll him over in the bed, and find him an empty orange-juice bottle. Checking his refrigerator on one of my visits, I found absolutely nothing in the way of nourishment.

This situation had to be addressed. Locating Ray's mother's phone number, I discussed his condition, and she agreed to look into it. The next day, an ambulance scooped Ray up and took him to a health-care facility, where I thought he would be in good hands.

It turned out that was not the case. The calls from Ray to me doubled to ten to fifteen per day. He was absolutely not happy with the place or the staff and wanted to come home. This went on for a week, and then I got a call from the facility at 3:00 a.m. Knowing from experience that this was not a good sign, I tried to find out what had happened, but the lady on the phone wouldn't share any information. She was trying to get a hold of Ray's family (really not good).

Around noon Ray's mom called me to tell me that Ray had committed suicide that night. He was so unhappy with his situation that life was unbearable. Mrs. Guidroz explained that Ray's Mensa-level brain fashioned a noose out of the call button chord, and he just fell out of bed, hanging himself in the process. Without the use of his limbs because of the unreported stroke he had shortly after arriving to the facility, Ray wouldn't have been able to change his mind. His inevitable death was the result he was seeking.

I am so sorry that I didn't know earlier about Ray's situation so I could have done something for him and got him the help which he so desperately needed. But he was such a private person that his family didn't even know. I can only promise to be more vigilant of my people in the future.

I'm sorry, Ray.

Naomi Muska was a ninety-something little old lady with the greenest thumb for gardening anyone has ever seen. She came to us from a ratty, nasty trailer park, where she had rented two spaces. One space was for her enormous three-bedroom single-wide. The other space was for all her plants.

She explained that the park where she lived had been condemned, and she needed a place for her home within thirty days. I told her I had nothing at the moment but would develop a site for her and her plants. I really wanted Naomi and her greenery.

She left me a deposit, and I began excavation of the new addition to our park, space number 36, with the promise to have it ready in thirty days. This was no easy task, not only supplying water/sewer, gas, and electric to an area, which never had it before, but also the area was on the side of a hill! Excavation of space number 36 went well, and so did the installation of all utilities, faster than the agreed-upon thirty days.

Soon Naomi was relocating her plants to her new home, making the place look great as I had hoped. Then her storage building, her carport, and finally her huge home were delivered. She and I were as happy as we could be: Naomi with all her plants, which she worked on every day, and me with a real showstopper of a space in our park.

For years Ms. Naomi continued to work the plants, making her spot a place to be proud of and giving her a purpose in life. Then one day we noticed she was spending less time in her yard. After all, she was in her late nineties for Pete's sakes. I decided to check in on her often, making sure she was all right. Each time I came by, she assured me that she was just a bit tired and was slowing down in her old age.

We had an agreement that she would leave the door unlocked so I could peek in and check on her. I kept this up for about six months, and I would always find her in her recliner, watching her favorite TV shows with a drink in her hand.

Then one day the door was locked. I had a bad feeling about this. Naomi had never failed to let me have access to check on her. Knocking on the door and all the front windows did no good. I began to worry.

Making my way to the back of the house, I broke into the master bathroom window. Nothing looked out of place—the bedroom looked neat as a pin. The kitchen was clean as a whistle. Then I saw her, as usual, sitting in her recliner in the living room. The TV was showing her favorite show, and she had a drink in her hand and a smile on her face. My voice got no response, so I checked for vitals.

Naomi had no pulse, and she was not breathing. What got me was she was warm to the touch. I truly believe she had just passed. When the EMTs got there, they confirmed what I thought. Naomi wasn't gone long from this world, but indeed she had passed on to the next.

I purchased the home at number 36 from Naomi's family, and it became our nicest rental. We always hoped a renter would attend to the planting areas Ms. Naomi had made. None ever did, but number

36 still has the most beautiful garden plantings in the park. Naomi lives on and is remembered by all the hard work she put into making our park a nice and beautiful place to live.

In Remembrance

- Rick Thrash: Stayed with us for many years in Al Roy's little farmhouse. He was a local realtor and managed a large exclusive housing development on the lake just down the street from us. Rick died a few years ago, cause unknown. I really wish newspaper obits would print cause of death.
- Darrell Holcome: Son of Karen Mckinney (whose story is in chapter 13); lived in our park for several years with his wife and young son. Darrell died of a motorcycle accident just down the road. He was not wearing a helmet.
- Sammie Hanna: Her boyfriend, Hollis, was a bullfighter on the weekends, and she was enough of a tomboy that I would not have been surprised if she had tried the sport as well. Sammie died of pancreatic cancer.
- Jean "Flo" Tankersely: Waited tables for many years at the Club Café in downtown Hot Springs. She drove a pretty red truck. Saw in the paper she had died. Her story is also in chapter 13.
- Paulette Spiva: Moved with us from our old park to our new one. Paulette was our rental deep cleaner and did an excellent job for us for many years. She died of cancer.
- Bobby Stewart: Boyfriend of Paulette, Bobby was a honky-tonker from a past life. He had been stabbed, shot, and beat up multiple times. He drove trucks and cabs and loved to drink and gamble. He was a true character and was also taken by cancer.
- Toni Jester Carpenter: She was one of our first residents of the second park, and I really enjoyed watching her work on her roof dressed in her short shorts. Toni was a victim of the COVID virus. I'm so sorry for her husband, Scott. Toni's (and Scott's) story is in chapter 4.

CHAPTER 16

Acknowledgments

You may have noticed the word "maybe" under the title of the last chapter. The conundrum I have with closing this book of stories is the fact I have piles of notes with fantastic, interesting, sad, and hilarious stories, which all occurred in my life. It seems I have left the people who have read the book, prepublished, wanting and demanding more. Another good reason to believe a follow-up book is in my future is the amazing amount of incidents and stories my tenants continue to furnish me almost on a daily basis. Every time I am presented with an unbelievable incident by one of my knuckleheaded tenants, I think that now I have seen everything. *Not!* Shortly thereafter, another outrageous happening occurs.

For these reasons, I feel it only right to acknowledge each and every tenant we've had stay with us over the past forty plus years. We love most of you and despise a few of you. Without you, most of this book would not have been possible.

I feel it very necessary to mention all the unnamed, unsuspecting victims sitting or lying around the pool on vacation in Mexico. Sorry for disturbing your downtime, but thanks for taking time to read my book. Also thanks for all your corrections and suggestions you left in the columns. Gracias!

To all my friends and family who said they read the book (who knows if they did) thanks for your interest and encouragement. A special thanks to friends, Mark Griffith, Rich Croome, Susan Hamre, Michelle Tremblay, and Manuel Guittet.

To my wife, Gay, who I know for sure did read the entire book, thank you so much. I know she read it because after I would finish a chapter or section, we would sit together, me with my feet up on the desk, while she read it back to me. Great inflection, my sweet baby Gay. I love you.

Last but for sure not least, thanks to my tennis buddy and editor, Bill Norby. He said his biggest problem has been staying focused and not getting distracted while laughing at these unimaginable tales! It is with great gratitude I thank Bill for taking on this impossible task.

Will there be a sequel?

ABOUT THE ILLUSTRATOR

Dr. Gary Simmons is a nationally recognized pen-and-ink artist. He has Gary Simmons Studio in Hot Springs, Arkansas. In 1992 he wrote *The Technical Pen: Techniques for Artists*, published by New York's Watson-Guptill Publishers and issued in English and translated in Chinese and Russian. The book grew out of his teaching pen-and-ink seminars for Rapidograph, the manufacturer of Simmons' pens. After going out of print in 2013, the book was republished by Echo Point Books in Vermont. He can be contacted at <u>penwizard1@gmail.com</u>. He is represented by Justus fine Art (dja@aristotle.net).

ABOUT THE AUTHOR

Gary Strakshus is a veteran in mobile home park management. His specialties include confrontation, repair of any part of any trailer, and choosing the correct renter for a specific rental. Gary's on the job training has stretched on for over forty-five years, and he is still finding solutions for problems of the park. This is Gary's debut novel. He lives with his wife in the mobile home village located in Hot Springs, Arkansas.

9 798888 960069 5